WORDS TO LIVE  GH BY

DENISE'S
DAILY
WORD

WORDS TO LIVE BY, LOVE BY & LAUGH BY

DENISE'S DAILY WORD

WRITTEN BY
DENISE Y. BARROW

SBI

STREBOR BOOKS
NEW YORK LONDON TORONTO SYDNEY

Strebor Books
P.O. Box 6505
Largo, MD 20792
www.simonandschuster.com

This book is a work of nonfiction.

ISBN 978-1-59309-618-2
ISBN 978-1-4767-9895-0 (ebook)
LCCN 2015957688

First Strebor Books trade paperback edition February 2016

Cover design: www.mariondesigns.com
Cover photograph: © Keith Saunders/Keith Saunders Photos
Interior photograph: © Triff/Shutterstock.com

10 9 8 7 6 5 4 3 2 1

Manufactured in the United States of America

For information regarding special discounts for bulk purchases,
please contact Simon & Schuster Special Sales at 1-866-506-1949

The Simon & Schuster Speakers Bureau can bring authors to your live event.
For more information or to book an event, contact the Simon & Schuster Speakers
Bureau at 1-866-248-3049 or visit our website at www.simonspeakers.com.

To God and His Will for my life

My personal daily verses, thoughts and prayers for us.
Enjoy.

✝ ✡ ☪ ☯

Therefore being justified by faith, we have peace with God through our Lord Jesus Christ. By whom also we have access by faith into this grace wherein we stand, and rejoice in hope of the Glory of God. And not only so, but we glory in tribulations also: knowing that tribulation worketh patience; And patience experience; and experience hope:

—ROMANS 5:1-4

THOUGHT:

Utilize your faith to overcome hindrances. Faith cannot alter purpose; it can, only acts as an agent to assist in fulfilling the predetermined purpose to God. There's nothing like time to show us that we have misplaced our priorities. I don't know about you but I wouldn't trust my future with anybody but God.

My personal testimonial prayer:

Father God, I thank You for allowing me, Denise Yvette Barrow, to witness and experience firsthand the power of exhibiting FAITH in Your Word, Faith in Your promises, Faith in my praise, Faith in my belief of YOU, Faith in my worship, and Faith in the love that You have placed in my heart for Your people. For I know, Lord, that if any of it was of me, this would be a different prayer. Lord, I believe and trust You for my life and the lives of those reading this prayer. Lord, only You know what we stand in need of. We thank You for Your delivering power, Your grace and mercy that You so freely give. I thank You for complete healing, finances, for a sound mind. I thank and praise You for the freedom from depression in Your people, for comfort and for peace. Oh Lord, I thank You for LIFE, life on earth and life everlasting. I choose to ask nothing of You, Father God. I just came to thank You today. I come today with the heart of prayer and praise of Thanksgiving. Though I am sick in my body, Lord Jesus, I believe You for my healing. I know I am making the enemy really mad at me right now, because he hates us to praise and worship You. I am FULLY persuaded that, what You promised, You are also able to perform it, in the Powerful Mighty Name of Jesus Christ, Our Lord. Amen.

✝ ✡ ☪ ☯

But if we walk in the light, as He is in the light, we have fellowship one with another, and the blood of Jesus Christ His Son cleanseth us from all sin.

— I JOHN 1:7

THOUGHT:

Imagine, if we walk according to how He/Jesus walked, we have fellowship with each other. If we take the time to look at the latter part of this scripture, the BLOOD of Jesus cleanseth us from ALL sin. First, we must understand that, when the suffix *eth* is attached to a word in the Bible, it means to continually occur. Therefore, when this scripture states the blood of Jesus cleanseth us from sin, this is a continuous act. It cleans you today and it will continue to cleanse you in the future. Take a biological look at blood. Through blood, we can tell who we belong to through DNA. So if we are covered and cleansed with the Blood of Christ and we are in Christ, this makes us one with Christ and joint heirs with Christ. Therefore, we are related through His blood. His Father becomes Abba Father (Our Father). This is why I can comfortably say that ALL on this list is my FAMILY! Without the Blood of Christ, we cease to have proof of our sonship to God. Yes, more on this list are my physical biological family, but, the Word teaches us that we are one through Christ. We are joint heirs with Christ, meaning ALL that He is entitled to, we are entitled to also. Wow, did ya'll hear me? I am feeling this, but let's go a little more deeper. I'm putting on my Registered Nurse cap for this one. We NEED blood in our bodies in order to live. It is the main element in our body that affects every part of our body. It carries oxygen, nutrients and healing factors (WBC, RBC, platelets) that are necessary to sustain life in EVERY cell of the body. If blood is restricted from any part of our body for a long period of time, that body part will die. Every part of the human body needs the blood. Are ya'll getting what I am saying to you? The physical body is illustrating the POWER of the BLOOD of the Body of Christ. Every member of the Body of Christ needs the life-giving Blood of Jesus. When DNA proves we are our natural father's children, saying and believing that we are covered through the blood of Christ, we now share the same father as Him. Know that, without the Blood of Christ, we are not true heirs but people who are trying to get the inheritance and promises of God reserved for the legitimate sons and daughters of God! I don't know about you, but I AM A LEGITIMATE DAUGHTER OF GOD. I am confident in my inheritance and I trust God for ALL of the promises that He has made to me. This is why being diagnosed with Stage 4 breast cancer NEVER beat me and it never will. God NEVER spoke it to my soul or spirit as my lot in life. He has made me some promises that I have yet to see and until I see and experience them ALL, I will be right here praising His Holy name and spreading His prophetic Word, praying for all of us to be covered in the Blood of Jesus. And believing and trusting that, as Frankie Beverly and Maze sings "We Are One." Praise God and thank Him for the Blood of the Lamb.

PRAYER:

Abba Father, which art in Heaven, we come to you daily with our hands lifted up and our hearts filled with praise. We know that it's your grace and mercy that has brought us through, but we have the understanding that it is the POWER of the Blood that sustains us. Lord, we ask for forgiveness for any and all sin, whether done in deed or thought, knowingly and unknowingly. Forgive us for unforgiveness. Forgive us, for not walking in love with one another as we are in this journey together as one big family in You. Lord, I thank You for everyone that shares the Word in their daily walk. Father, You have given me the esteem pleasure to have people in my life that show me a piece of You every day. Thank You, Lord, for love, peace, understanding, humility, the Blood of the Lamb and the blood that runs through my veins. Father, thank You for all that fear You and keep Your statutes. Thank You for loving us enough to allow us another day to get it right. It is in Jesus' Name that I pray. Amen and Amen!

✝ ✡ ☾ ☯

VERSE:

Though he were a Son, yet learned he obedience by the things which he suffered.

—HEBREWS 5:8

But as for you, ye thought evil against me; but God has meant it unto good, to bring to pass.

—GENESIS 50:20

Ye are of God, little children, and have overcome them: because greater is he that is in you, than he who is in the world.

—1 JOHN 4:4

THOUGHT:

Go through your go through! Count it all Joy. You are going through what you are going through or went through to be a blessing to someone who WILL go through the same thing. Depending on how you handle your go through can determine and enable someone to come out of the situation or prevent them from going through at all. A wise, younger cousin of mine (Sheryl) recently told me, the way I handled the death of my daughter gave her the strength to deal with the loss of her daughter (Storm). I initially looked at her like she lost her mind, because I was a hot mess when Nyleve did not survive her life. Sheryl reminded me that for years she has watched the way in which I live my life, that I have survived a lot of adversity with a smile, joke and love in my heart. To her the mere fact that though I wanted to die and attempted to make that happen, that was over twenty years ago, I am still here. The mere fact that I suffered near-death experiences with my asthma and now the cancer, she stated she has watched me and admired my strength and I am still here. NOTHING BUT THE GRACE OF GOD, through me and my faith, helped her through her go through. All of this was said to me during her daughter's funeral and I can proudly say that Sheryl is living a great walk of faith in our Lord, she is at peace and she is STILL here. Storm's father eloquently gave Sheryl peace by saying to her, that she named her Storm as storms come through with strong winds, make an impact, then leave. Family, don't pray away your storms, walk through them, cry through them, pray through them, stand still if need be, but whatever you do, go through them. When God wants to do a work in you and your life, He will put you in a place of aloneness. At this time He will begin to speak to you. It is up to you to take heed to your storm and take the time in the quiet place to hear from God. Try NOT to miss the opportunity God is taking/putting you aside in order for you to hear from Him and be obedient to Him. God's Word is a mirror to you and a mirror doesn't lie. You see what you see. You have every idea of what you are dealing with in the mirror. It's when you begin to change what you see, the problems and lies come about. You'll begin to talk differently, think differently, act differently, walk differently, choose your friends differently and you will even begin to praise God differently. So look at yourself in the mirror and notice your change when you begin to feed yourself the Word of God. In the midst of your mess and change, continue to praise God. The time it takes for your change to come is up to you. God already knows His plans for you and the timing of his plans. The longer you take to become obedient to God's Word and laws, the longer it will take for your change to come about. Only God can fix you. Realize that disobedience causes delays of all kinds of things; blessings, healings, transformation and victories. Just because these things can be delayed, it doesn't mean they will be denied. Begin to learn obedience through your sufferings. Know that what the enemy means for your bad, God WILL turn it out for your good. This I have found to be true for myself: greater is He that is IN me than he (me) that is in the world. I take this scripture to mean me being in Christ is far greater than me being in the world, living my life any ol' kind of way. I also take it to mean that the God that is inside of me is far greater than the enemy of this world, which is anything and anybody that is contrary to God and His laws. My God is an awesome God; He reigns in heaven and earth.

PRAYER:

Lord, I come to You today with a loving, open, pure heart. I thank You, that I am living in the fullness of You. Lord, I pray that we learn that our obedience is the cause of our blessings, change and growth in You. Lord, I ask that You break the curse of people being connected to others who have empowered themselves to fail, for those connected to them will fail as well. I thank You for Your Word that You have imparted into us. It has proven to be the greatest gift given to man. Lord, I ask that all of the dreams and visions of Your people be manifested moment by moment. As we walk in obedience to Your call of us to You and Your ways, protect us from the wiles, tricks and traps of the enemy. If it is Your Will that we have to go through, I thank You in advance for it. I thank You for what the enemy sets out to kill, steal and destroy, You have placed a protective hedge around me and turned it into the best experience of my life. It was in the storms, the valleys, the deep pits and darkness that I learned who I am in You. Lord, I know that You desire to bless us and I thank You in advance for all that You provide when my mind is stayed on You. I can't thank You enough for Your peace, love, understanding, pardons, grace, mercy, blessings, healing, patience, chastisements, flat-out whippings/whoppings and delays. I will never forget ALL that You've done for me. I pray for Your people as well as myself this morning in the name of Jesus Your Son, my joint Heir, my Savior. Amen.

✝ ✡ ☾ ☯

VERSE:

Now the just shall live by faith: but if any man draw back, my soul shall have no pleasure in him.

—HEBREWS 10:38

THOUGHT:

Know that the value of faith is not about your lifestyle. As most people that God healed and dealt with were sinners. BUT, they were healed and drawn to Him because they believed. They had FAITH. The thing that moves God is faith. You must believe God! God will move in your life according to your faith, not your experience.

PRAYER:

Father God, in Your infinite wisdom, I come to You today asking you to help Your people with their faith. You said all we need it to be, is that of the size of a mustard seed. Forgive them for any lack of faith that they exhibit. I trust and believe You are who You say that You are. Our Mighty Counselor, our Comforter, our Keeper, our Protector, our Provider, our Prince of Peace, our King of Kings and our Lord of Lords. Keep us in Your presence as we begin to see and experience the manifestation of You in our lives. In the mighty name of Jesus, I pray. Amen.

✝ ✡ ☪ ☯

VERSE:

And whatsoever ye shall ask in my name, that will I do, that the Father may be glorified in the Son. If ye shall ask any thing in my name, I will do it.

—JOHN 14:13-14

THOUGHT:

God will give you whatever you ask for. You must first ask. You also have to be careful of what you ask for. Not everything you want and ask for is what is best for you. Therefore, don't get upset if you asked for something and you received it and it didn't quite work out the way YOU hoped it would. It may not have been a part of what God wanted for you. But He is a keeper of His word and you asked for it, so, He obliged you. Know that He will give you a business, He will give you a dream and He will make you the head and not the tail. Believe God for your household. Believe God for your deliverance. Believe God for your purpose. And believe that WHATEVER you ask of Him you will receive it.

PRAYER:

Heavenly Father, I come to You today humble in your presence as Your child by faith in Christ Jesus. I thank You for strength when the storms of life are raging. I thank You for giving Your people the desires of our hearts. I ask that You help us to stand in the liberty of the freedom that You have given to us. I come to You as a believer, believing that whatever I ask for in Jesus' name, I will receive it. Father God, I ask that You bless the people on this prayer list and whomever they share Your word with. Give them all that they ask for above what they could ever imagine or foresee according to Your Will and Your Word. I thank You for Your grace and mercy as You continue to finish the work that You began in us. In Jesus' precious name, I pray. Amen.

✝ ✡ ☪ ☯

*O GIVE thanks to the Lord, for He is good. His love endures forever.
O give thanks unto the God of heaven: for His mercy endureth forever.*
—PSALM 136:1 AND 26

THOUGHT:

Our thanks rise from the nature of God and His glory and goodness. The reason we give thanks is because God is good and His love is inexhaustible, beyond decay, and neverending. God is God all by Himself; He doesn't need our help. His mercy is new every day for us and it lasts beyond our last breath. There is NO end to God's grace, mercy or love toward us.

PRAYER:

O great Lover of my soul, thank You for sending Jesus as the demonstration of Your love. I love you, Father. I love You for who You are and what You have done. I love You for what You have promised. I love You for the blessings You shower upon me. I love You for giving me hope. I love You because You first loved me. I love You because You gave Your only begotten Son, so that I may LIVE. I love You because You are worthy of all love. But, I confess that my love is not as strong as Yours. I desire to exhibit the kind of unconditional love toward Your people that You so effortlessly do daily. Please, fill me with Your love by the power of the Holy Spirit. Through Jesus I lift up my heart to You. Amen.

✝ ✡ ☪ ☯

VERSE:

If my people, which are called by my name, shall humble themselves, and pray, and seek my face, and turn from their wicked ways; then will I hear from heaven, and will forgive their sin and heal their land.

—2 CHRONICLES 7:14

THOUGHT:

I don't know a better time than today to get on your knees, stand in your closet, sit down with your hands clasped, whatever, wherever or however you do it, it is time to have the most powerful prayer life imaginable. The times we are living in, is cause to put on the whole armor of God and begin to speak to the Father. As you seek His Will for your life, our loving Father said that whatsoever you ask in His Son's name you shall receive it. But in order to have this happen, we must first humble ourselves. We must want to come out of purposeful sin. That is, sin that you know you're committing. God is calling for His children to stand in the gap for one another and when we do that, He will do ALL that we desire of Him to do for us. He will heal the world of its ills.

PRAYER:

Holy Father, the lover of my soul, I come to You as your child. First giving honor and all praises due to You. Asking that You forgive me of any sin in my life. Anything that I have said, done or thought of, that was not of You, I ask that You forgive me. As this world has major ills, I ask that Your will be done in Your people. I come to You today praying for my family, Your children, that they might know Your power and the power of their prayers. Lord, I know that my prayers and my belief of what I pray will come to pass. Lord, I ask that You continue to be a keeper of my life, mind, body, soul and spirit. Father, I ask that You bless all that will pray this prayer and share this prayer with others. In Jesus' precious name, Amen.

✝ ✡ ☪ ☯

VERSE:

Trust in the Lord with all thine heart; and lean not unto thine own understanding. In all thy ways acknowledge him, and he shall direct thy paths.

—PROVERBS 3:5-6

THOUGHT:

Discouragement comes when people feel they've seen it all and most of it was terrible. No matter how old you are, you haven't seen it all. No one knows how God will end His book. He is the Author and Finisher of your life. What I do know is that He saves the best for last. As He said it in His Word, the first shall be the last and the last shall be the first. It's not a good look to assume that what you will see out of life will be similar to what you saw before. Hold on, God has a way of restoring purpose to your life. The very one you are trying to send away, may have the key to restoring purpose and fulfillment to your life. Keep the faith and trust GOD!

PRAYER:

Lord, I thank You for being an all-knowing, omnipotent, loving God. I thank You because You and You alone know my fate. You knew my beginning and my end before I was conceived in my mother's womb. You knew I would be right here, at this moment, sending out Your Word to Your people. Father, I promise, not even for one second, to think I can understand anything that occurs in my life. Instead, I will lean on Your Holy Word and Holy Spirit to lead and guide me on my way. In all that I say and do, I will lift You up. You are the potter and I am the clay. Mold me and make me into who You predestined me to be. With the love You have shown and given me, I will intercede on the behalf of those who don't know You, for those who are weary and for those who have lost their way. I pray that they come to know you in a mighty way. In the name of Jesus, I pray. Amen!

✝ ✡ ☾ ☯

The thief cometh not, but for to steal, and to kill, and to destroy: I am come that they may have life, and that they may have it more abundantly.

—John 10:10

For his anger endureth but a moment; in his favour is life: weeping may endure for a night but joy cometh in the morning.

—Psalm 30:5

THOUGHT:

Jesus came to the world to give us life. He didn't come to bring us rules, judgment, fear, or work. Jesus came to give us life in its fullest form, abundance. Although we know that life in abundance is promised to us when we go to be with Him for all eternity, we need to understand that Jesus' promise to give us life begins right now! Not JUST life later, but also life NOW! There will unfortunately be bad nights at one time or another in your lives. The good news is there will be a morning after. Allow the joy of the morning light to push away any unwanted partners, curses, people or fears that stop you from achieving your goals. Feed what you want to live/flourish in your life and starve what you want to die. God has given you enough food in His Word to live life today and live it more abundantly. I charge all of us to LIVE now and let all that is in your lives that is plaguing you, to not feed that thing and let it die. That includes ill relationships, ill job situations, illnesses, unruly children, your negative thoughts, past hurts and your personal inner struggles.

PRAYER:

Almighty God, I confess that sometimes I play life too carefully, not risking failure and loss and not reaching for your opportunities and your concerns. Give me a heart that yearns to live life in all its fullness by seeking after Your Will, Jesus' example and the Holy Spirit's leading in my decisions today, and always. Let Your light shine on me and may Your peace forever be upon me. May Your love and wisdom always lead and guide my way. Lord, continue to give me the faith I need to make my dreams come true. God, let Your unconditional love, grace, peace and joy reside with everyone praying this prayer today. Lord, protect us from all things and people that come to harm, kill and destroy our minds, bodies, spirits and souls, through the name of Jesus, I ask this to Your glory. Amen.

✝ ✡ ☾ ☯

VERSE:

Though he slay me, yet will I trust him: but I will maintain mine own ways before him. He also shall be my salvation: for a hypocrite shall not come before him.

—Job 13:15-16

THOUGHT:

Things may be going totally haywire in your life right now: You may be going through afflictions, heartache, broken marriages, loss of a loved one, unemployment, being overwhelmed, walking in darkness, abuse, childhood demons, confusion, low self-esteem and disbelief. The bottom line is that if you profess to know and love God, then you must trust Him with ALL aspects of your life. Yes, that means the good, the bad, and the ugly. Realize that many of the issues you may be dealing with are often rooted in the ashes of your childhood. You must begin or continue to rely on the Word of God, who alone knows your beginning to your end. Note that God is not pleased with hypocrites. As it is hypocritical of you to say that you believe and trust God for ALL things but you don't want to recognize that when certain issues arise, you begin to doubt God and not stand on faith for the God you profess to serve. Also, stop quoting scripture; I can do all things in Christ which strenghteneth me. God just cannot be your all in all only when things are all good. If He is your all in all, then through the bad you will stand in the same manner that you stand when things are good. Stand in His presence strong, with courage, with joy and thanksgiving. God deals in truth, as you see Job stating his truth/circumstances. He did not say his wife or his backstabbing friends slayed him. He states, though God slayed him, afflicted him, took all that he had, from his children to his wealth, that even through ALL of THAT, he would trust God for his end. We all know what Job's end was. Marinate on that! Thank you, Lord. Therefore, no matter what your truth is, God knows all about it. All you need to do is trust that He will see you through it.

PRAYER:

Dear Lord, hear my prayer. Please do not hide Your face from me during these troubling times. As with David, hear my call unto You and answer me quickly. I need a divine intervention. I need NOTHING short of a miracle. I have been a great comfort to others, but Father, You are the True Comforter. People are reaching out to me with issues greater than I could ever handle without Your guidance. I Thank You for giving me a word to keep them encouraged. Father, households, marriages, MINDS, bodies, finances, spirits and souls are being waged upon. I understand that it is the enemy's job to kill, steal and destroy Your people. As he is on his job 24/7, I desire to be on mine for equal time, un-wavering. Lord, I have no complaints in You. I love You and pray for strength to continue to be a blessing to others, to stand with faith and courage to share Your Word with the world. I count all that I ask done, in the Mighty name of Jesus. Amen.

✝ ✡ ☪ ☯

For I know the thoughts that I think toward you, saith the Lord, thoughts of peace, and not evil, to give you an expected end.

—JEREMIAH 29:11

THOUGHT:

NO one can hear God think, but we can feel the effects of His thoughts toward us. If God's thoughts of you are ALL good and none of evil, why do you have negative thoughts of yourself? Clear your mind of dead things so that you can feed the seeds of greatness that is in the womb of your mind that is for growth and LIFE!!!

PRAYER:

Holy Father above, I come to You today to ask You to help us to know who we are in You. Allow me to lead the life You have purposed my birth for. Father God, I thank You for my expected end, which gives me joy and peace. The devil thought he had me, but I thank You for putting him in his place. I know that thoughts are powerful and that they can nurse negative insecurities that limit us and exempt us from greatness. I ask that You take these thoughts out of Your people's minds. Lord, grant us tranquil, peaceful and successful thoughts that build positive character in heart. As we believe our expected end to be nothing less than successful, we ask these things in prayer, in the Mighty Name of Jesus. Amen.

✝ ✡ ☪ ☯

The spirit of the Lord hath made me, and the breath of the almighty hath given me life.

—JOB 33:4

Yea, though I walk through the valley of death, I will fear no evil: for thou art with me; thy rod and thy staff they comfort me.

—PSALM 23:4

THOUGHT:

Here we see two different men professing the same thing about their situations. Job was surely going through the valley of death, and when he made his declaration that God made him and gave him life, he was talking to nonbelievers. He let them know no matter what he was going through, he would trust the Potter/God as he was clay ready to be molded in whatever fashion God deemed he needed to be made. Whatever the process, valley, or go through, he was going to go through it without fear. David, on the other hand, had to encourage his own heart for his belief of God for his life. He knew he was a messed up dude, but no matter how much or how many times he messed up, he was determined to go to God for help to get it right. Both clearly understood we are not in this thing called life all willy-nilly by ourselves. God is with us every step of the way. It is up to us to believe and proceed with trust and not fear. NO matter what you go through, your valley, your ups or your downs, live it trusting God without fear. I tell you, when God gives you life, NOTHING and NO ONE can take it away. Because we are believers, we all understand that God is with us in IT ALL. He grants us comfort in dangerous situations and we must trust God for our expected end, through our valley, without fear, we are here to say to that mange the devil, "WE ARE STILL HERE," for it is God who has made us and given us life and ONLY GOD will come to get us, at His appointed time!!!!!!!!!!!! Praise God for He is good.

PRAYER:

Lord, I come to You today with a gracious heart filled with thanksgiving. I know that by Your grace I am still here. Lord, I thank You for my go through, for I know that You instructed me to count IT ALL JOY. You didn't say what the IT would be, but I count every good and bad thing joy. I love You for loving and trusting me enough that I would trust and stand for You in my most trying of times. Thank You for sparing life and covering us with Your protective will over our lives. Lord, as I know things can be worse in every life that I feed Your Word to, I thank You for giving us what we need to survive IT, to overcome IT, to live through IT, and to have the VICTORY over IT. Thank You, we love You, we trust You, and don't fear anything the devil conjures up to destroy us. We stand together, we stand apart, but most importantly, we stand with You. In the precious name of Jesus, I pray. Amen.

✝ ✡ ☪ ☯

This next verse is a self-explanatory Psalm, so I have no thoughts about it. I leave the thought to you all. For I know once you read it, you will have more thought than you can handle. Remember, this walk we are taking with the Father is PERSONAL.

VERSE:

HE that dwelleth in the secret place of the most High shall abide under the shadow of the Almighty. I will say of the Lord, He is my refuge and my fortress: my God; in him will I trust. Surely he shall deliver thee from the snare of the fowler, and from the noisome pestilence. He shall cover thee with his feathers, and under his wings shalt thou trust: his truth shall be thy shield and buckler. Thou shalt not be afraid for the terror by night; nor by the arrow that flieth by day; Nor for the pestilence that walketh in darkness; nor for the destruction that wasteth at noonday. A thousand shall fall at thy side, and ten thousand at thy right hand; but it shall not come nigh thee. Only with thine eyes shalt thou behold and see the reward of the wicked. Because thou hast made the Lord, which is my refuge, even the most High, thy habitation; There shall no evil befall thee, neither shall any plague come nigh thy dwelling. For he shall give his angels charge over thee, to keep thee in all thy ways. They shall bear thee up in their hands, lest thou dash thy foot against a stone. Thou shalt tread upon the lion and adder; the young lion and the dragon shalt thou trample under feet. Because he hath set his love upon me, therefore will I be deliver him: I will set him on high, because he hath known my name. He shall call upon me, and I will answer him: I will be with him in trouble; I will deliver him, and honour him. With long life will I satisfy him, and shew him my salvation.

—PSALM 91:1-16

PRAYER:

Lord, I come to You due to Your loving kindness, praising Your Holy name. Thank You for giving comfort in Your Word and promises toward me and my life. Thank You for being my refuge in all that try to attack my mind, body, soul, and spirit. Thank You for sending your angels that I experience here on earth in spirit and in human form. Thank You for all the people on this list and their families. Lord, we desire to be on one accord and that is to love, trust, and believe in You. Thank You for loving me and answering my prayers. Father, I thank You for salvation and deliverance. Thank You for being my all and all. I thank You for Your word as it is a blueprint for the life that You've given me. I know that if I am stuck on an answer to a situation in my life, I have Your Word to fall back on for the answers. I desire to know You more daily. Increase You in my life and decrease me. Lord, I know at times I get in Your way but I thank You for being a loving Father, for gently taking me out of my own way and, when I am being hard headed, doing whatever it takes to move me out of my own way. Thank You, for I am glad to know Your name and thank You that, in spite of me, You STILL CALL MY NAME. In Jesus' name, I pray. Amen.

✝ ✡ ☪ ☯

THEREFORE thou art inexcusable, O man, whosoever thou art that judgest: for wherein thou judgest another, thou condemest thyself; for thou that judgest does the same things. But we are sure that the judgment of God is according to truth against them which commit such things.

—Romans 2:1-2

For all have sinned and come of the glory of God.

—Romans 3:23

THOUGHT:

Do you know people (could be you) that find fault with everybody? This person is always late, the store clerk is always slow, so and so is always rude, the minister is boring, people are too loud, too quiet, too fat, too skinny, too immoral, too prudish, too this or too that. In some of our eyes no one is really worth much at all. Forgiveness is a word that is not found in some people's vocabulary. They just can't forgive people for being human. They can't forgive people for doing the very things that they do themselves. Lucky for us, God does acknowledge our humanness and He loves us just the same. God has yet to see the perfect human being, apart from Jesus. But that doesn't change His love and forgiveness toward us. When we begin to see others as well as ourselves through the eyes of God's love, then we find that we can accept and love others, as well as ourselves just the way that we are. We must live according to God's Word for us—judge not least you be judged. A just man falleth (which means continually) 7 times 7. God clearly lets us know that we ALL have sinned and come short of His glory, His expectations, His purpose for us. Therefore, when we judge others, ultimately we are placing that same scrutiny on ourselves.

PRAYER:

Lord, I come before You with my hands and face lifted up toward You, asking You to help me to first accept who I am that I may be able to accept others exactly as they are. Destroy in me the tendency to be judgmental. Father God, teach me new ways to affirm others and spread Your grace. I ask that You help me find the lovable in all people as I face that challenge every day with the different people I encounter daily. Lord, give me compassion that gives the power to build up rather than tear down Your people. Lord, I know You may not approve of my conduct but I thank You for loving me anyway. Thank You for Your Word and giving me grace that I may not pass judgment on any one, even myself. I have faith that all that I ask I count it done in the precious name of Jesus. Amen.

✝ ✡ ☪ ☯

VERSE:

To everything there is a season, and a time to every purpose under the heaven: A time to be born, and a time to die; a time to plant, and a time to pluck up that which is planted;

—ECCLESIASTES 3:1-2

THOUGHT:

We will always have seasons of struggles and testing. No one is exempt. There are times when EVERYTHING we attempt to do will seem to go wrong. Regardless of our prayer life or our consecration, our adversities will come. No, we can't pray away God's seasons, for they are His will for our lives. In the valley is where we seek God more. It is where we make better attempts at searching ourselves to make much needed changes. No matter how hard the storm is, we must still trust God. There is always a purpose for our temporary inconveniences, knowing that this too shall pass. Note, that some things are not meant for us to change, but are meant for us to survive. These setbacks allow for fresh commitment and renewal. Eventually, what you plant or put your time into, you will have the opportunity to reap what you've sown. If you only sow into your business, then you can't cry when you are successful but you have NO one to share that success with. If you sow into your family, you will be rich beyond measure, because more than you alone can become a success. It becomes continual by generations. We all are aware that we are born to die. There is the appointed time of life given to us through our birth to our living and there is an appointed time to our death. No one knows the time but God. There is no need to try to figure it out; all we need to concern ourselves with is how do we get to live for all eternity. You can do this in the flesh by procreation of a family tree/legacy of life or through the spirit through Christ. In Him we have eternal life. As long as we know that we will go through seasons, we need to prepare ourselves for the best conditions as well as the worst conditions.

PRAYER:

Lord, give me patience to weather any storm that may come my way. Allow me to be at peace with whatever season I am going through. In spite of the trials and tribulations that I face, I will trust You. Father, I thank You for the times You allow me to be fruitful and I thank You for the valley moments. Because it is in those moments that I gain perspective. Lord, help me to seek You more whether I am in the valley or on the mountaintop. Thank You for teaching me through Your Word, that the trying of my faith brings about patience. Allow me the ability to stand no matter what the season. Lord, I love You for always being available to me. In Jesus' name, I pray. Amen.

✝ ✡ ☪ ☯

VERSE:

Only let your conversation be as it becometh the gospel of Christ: that whether I come and see you, or else be absent, I may hear of your affairs, that ye STAND fast in one spirit, with one mind striving together for the faith of the gospel; And in NOTHING terrified by your adversaries: which is to them an evident token of perdition, but to you of salvation, and that of God. For unto you it is given in the behalf of Christ, not only to believe on him, but also to SUFFER for his sake.

—PHILIPPIANS 1:27-29

As ye have therefore received Christ Jesus the Lord, so walk ye in him: Rooted and built up in him, and established in the faith, as ye have been taught, abounding therein with thanksgiving. Beware lest any man spoil you through philosophy and vain deceit, after the tradition of men, after the rudiments of the world, and not after Christ. For in him dwelleth all the fullness of the Godhead bodily. And ye are COMPLETE in him, which is the HEAD OF ALL PRINCIPALITY and POWER:

—COLOSSIANS 2:6-10

Rejoice evermore. Pray without ceasing. In everything give thanks: for this is the will of God in Christ Jesus concerning you. Quench not the spirit. Despise not prophesyings. Prove all things; hold fast that which is good.

—1 THESSALONIANS 5:16-21

But thou hast fully known my doctrine, manner of life, purpose, faith, longsuffering, charity, patience, Persecutions, afflictions, which came unto me at Antioch, at Iconium, at Lystra; what persecutions I endured: but out of them all the Lord delivered me. Yea, and ALL that live Godly in Christ Jesus SHALL SUFFER PERSECUTION.

— II TIMOTHY 3:10-12

Just a prayer with no thought, for His Word is Mighty and Powerfully Clear.

PRAYER:

Lord, we come to You with heavy hearts, believing Your Word and are in total agreement with Your Word. I believe that I can do ALL things through Christ Jesus who strengthens me. Therefore, whatever the enemy throws my way, I know that I will receive the VICTORY!! Father, I need for You to work all situations out in Your people. Give us the strength to endure any trial until we are Victorious. Let the truth prevail, as the truth sets captives free. For in well doing, oftentimes great harm is endured. Father God, don't allow our good works to go unnoticed. The same that we have given to others give us back tenfold. Allow people to stand in the gap for one another. For I know in You we will endure trials and tribulations. I know that You are a mighty deliverer and a way maker. Provide Your protection over Your people, Lord, cover us in Your precious blood. I am confident that what You have begun as good work in me and those that love You, You will perform it until the day of Christ Jesus. I thank You, I love You, Lord, and I count it done in Jesus' Holy name. Amen.

✝ ✡ ☪ ☯

A little twist for the strong in faith, Greetings, may peace be unto you all, Assalamu Alaykum, The Lord has led me to not forget my family who receive my prayers along with His Word on a daily basis with love, open minds and open hearts. With that said, I am paying homage for the next entries to my other family members who are Muslim. (though we keep them covered) They have taught me to have the greatest of acceptance of others and have fed my prayer life by giving me scriptures from the Bible as well as the Quran for words of life, wisdom, knowledge and encouragement. They support and applaud my walk with Jesus, my Lord, as they see my light shine amongst men. They have prayed for me and trusted in my faith in which I stand in the liberty of freedom. I am charging all of you to remain spiritually minded as our Word tells and teaches us to be.

✝ ✡ ☪ ☯

VERSE:

BEHOLD, how good and how pleasant it is for brethren to dwell together in unity! It is like the precious ointment upon the head, that ran down upon the beard, even Aaron's beard: that went down to the skirts of his garments; As the dew of Her'-mon, and as the dew that descended upon the mountains of Zion: for there the Lord commanded the blessing, even life for evermore.

—PSALM 133:1-3

And when all the children of Israel saw how fire came down, and the glory of the Lord upon the house, they bowed themselves with their faces to the ground upon the pavement, and worshipped, and praised the Lord, saying. For he is good; and his mercy endureth forever.

—2 CHRONICLES 7:3

HAVE mercy upon me, O God, according to thy loving kindness: according unto the multitude of thy tender mercies blot out my transgressions.

—PSALM 51:1

AYAT:

Surah 11 Hud I'D 90

And ask forgiveness of your Lord, then turn to Him. Surely my Lord is Merciful, Loving-kind.

TRANSLATION OF MAULANA MUHAMMAD ALI
4TH EDITION QURAN

Meditating scriptures:
Isaiah 55:7, Jeremiah 33:8-9

THOUGHT:

I have been hearing a lot of controversy over religion in my lifetime, but more so when I got saved. But the God I serve doesn't allow me to judge a man/woman for their free choice of whom they will serve. As for me and my house, I will serve the Lord. This, to me, is a PERSONAL spiritual journey. A journey we as a people can and will take together, but it is personal for each of us. Putting religion aside, of what I gather from the Quran, it is conveying what the Bible states in scripture after scripture. We must ask the Lord for forgiveness of our sins. We must turn to Him and ask this of Him, in order for Him to hear us. Acknowledging God's mercy and loving kindness toward us, we believe He forgives us, even though we are a mess. I am glad for the level of spirituality in my family. Every interaction, lesson, teachings through the grace of my Father above, has molded me into the woman, daughter, sister, cousin, aunt, friend and wife that I am today. I have tried the spirit by the spirit and I am well pleased with all whom I share my life with daily. I honor God for sharing you all with me. I desire to live my life in LOVE, not in judgment. DO YOU?

PRAYER:

Father God, I thank You for the vision You have given me to embark on this path this week. Thank You for unity to unite Your people to come together in spirit, not Religion. You have been doing this in my life, ever since I was born. I continue to magnify the God that I serve. I thank You, Lord, for the days that I made Salah, wore kimahs and gained the understanding of modesty, a disciplined prayer life, covering up, for all of me was for You, Father

God. Thank You for giving me the choice of life or death, as I choose to LIVE. We come together to honor You, Our Father, Our Creator, Our ALL in All. We come to You today, asking forgiveness, if we have not shown love to any of Your children for any reason. Lord, open our hearts and minds to help us to be accepting of one another's views and choices. They may not be a choice either of us would make for ourselves but a choice You have allowed us to make nonetheless. Thank You for this Country, that I may worship You openly in freedom and in truth. Let Your light so shine in all of Your people, that we are living Your greatest commandment and that is to love one another UNCONDITIONALLY. To love one another as we love ourselves. God, You know, I loves me some me! Father, I trust in Your Word and Your Will, for Your people. In thy Word, Lord, make us one; in Your Word, Lord, we are one. In Jesus' name, I pray. Amen and Amen!

✝ ✡ ☪ ☯

VERSE:

Pilate said unto him, What is truth? And when he said this, he went out again unto the Jews, and saith unto them, I find in him no fault at all.

—JOHN 18:38

A false witness that speaketh lies, and he that soweth discord among brethren.

—PROVERBS 6:19

For my mouth shall speak truth; and wickedness is an abomination to my lips.

—PROVERBS 8:8

AYAT:

2nd Surah The Cow ÍD 42
And mix not up truth with falsehood, nor hide the truth while you know.

—TRANSLATION OF MAULANA MUHAMMAD ALI
4TH EDITION QURAN.

Meditation Scriptures:
2 Timothy 3:5, 2 Corinthians 4:1-3, Ephesians 5:1-2, 8-12, Psalm 52:3, 1 John 1:5-10

THOUGHT:

Throughout the Bible, there are plenty of scriptures that deal with the issue of knowing the truth, sharing the truth and having nothing to do with anything that is false, or a lie. We see the scripture of the Quran address this. We see Pilate within this dialogue trying his best to tell the Jews that he didn't find fault in Jesus, he asked them over and over wasn't Jesus the King of the Jews, all that Jesus said was found to be true, but they didn't want to hear it or say it, even though they knew it to be true. So in this case, they knew the truth but didn't stand up for the truth. Pilate attempted to give them an opportunity to stand by the truth, but he too failed to protect the truth that he knew. Our challenge as humans is, to keep with the truth that we know, to share that truth and restrain from lying, liars or false storytellers. How do we coexist with people who are sinners and "we" are not? I placed quotation marks around "we" because if we truly believe we are without sin, then the truth is not in us. This is true, not only because it says it in the Word, but we KNOW who we are, we are as filthy rags, we are born into sin, sin that we desire not to do; we find ourselves doing it anyway. How do we coexist with those that have totally different beliefs than we do? Is God telling us that we are to have nothing to do with our children if they decide to worship Buddha, Allah, God, Jehovah, Jesus Christ because we are practicing another religion? The question is presented, what does light have in common with darkness? How can two walk together if they aren't in agreement with one another? Does Our Lord view us this way? Does God not want to have anything to do with us if we are contrary to what He predestined us to be?

I leave you with this. The Word states that I am to love my neighbors, it does not say only love Christians because I am a Christian; only love women because I am a woman; only love black people/American black people because that is who I am. I particularly love the fact that I LOVE my people, unconditionally!!!!!!

PRAYER:

Lord, help me to speak Your truth. Be a lamp unto my feet, my thoughts, my heart and my way of life. Help me to remove sin from my life and anything that is not like You, remove it from me. Lord, I desire to be like You. Thank You for loving me, in spite of who I am, what I do, what I think or what I may say. Lord, allow me to be a witness to Your truth. Allow my walk with You to be a worthy example of Your Will in my life. Father God, we need peace amongst Your people. Thank You for family and our differences of thoughts, beliefs, choices, religious faith and lifestyles. These differences allow us the ability to love one another in spite of our religion. I pray all that have come under the subjection of this prayer begin to love unconditionally, without judgment, knowing that You are our only judge on that great day, that You are the beginning and the end. That You are the truth, the way, the light and our LIFE. I honor You today and forever more. In the name of Jesus, I pray. Amen.

I pray these verses find us all in a forward path toward love, peace, understanding, acceptance, support and tolerance of all of God's children. (You may want to take some time for this next entry. Subject matter is long but worth it.)

✝ ✡ ☾★ ☯

VERSE:

If ye fulfill the royal law according to the scripture, Thou shalt love thy neighbor as thyself, ye do well: But if ye have respect of persons, ye commit sin, and are convinced of the law as transgressors.

—JAMES 2:8-9

For there are no respect of persons with God.

—ROMANS 2:11

This is the entire first chapter/part of the Quran. It is titled, appropriately, "THE OPENING: Al-Fatihah." It is spoken of as *"Fatihat al-Kitab"* and it is a saying that the Prophet Muhammad *(may peace and blessings be upon him)* said that no prayer is complete without the recitation of *Fatihat al-Kitab.*

AL QUARAN; Part I; Chapter I
THE OPENING: Al-Fatihah
In the name of ALLAH, the Beneficent, the Merciful.
1. Praise be to ALLAH, the Lord of the worlds,
2. The Beneficent, the Merciful,
3. Master of the day of Requital.
4. Thee do we serve and Thee do we beseech for help.
5. Guide us on the right path,

6. *The path of those upon whom Thou hast bestowed favors,*
7. *Not those upon whom wrath is brought down, nor those who go astray.*
AMIN.

(TRANSLATION BY MAULANA MUHAMMAD 'ALI)

✝ ✡ ☪ ☯

The first three verses of this surah *speak of the grandeur of GOD and the last three of the aspiration of man's soul to attain spiritual loftiness, while the middle verse, speaks of the relationship of man to the Divine Spirit. In this* surah, *it is pointed out through which man can attain to real greatness. It is through* obedience *combined with complete humility, and through seeking help from GOD. The idea of service or worship in Islam is not a mere declaration of the glory to GOD, but the imbibing of Divine morals and receiving their impress through humble service to GOD; hence the prayer for Divine help.*

VERSE:

O Lord, our Lord how excellent is thy name in all the earth! Who hast set thy glory above the heavens.

—PSALM 8:1

And they that know thy name will put their trust in thee: for thou, Lord, hast not forsaken them that seek thee.

—PSALM 9:10

Thou wilt shew me the path of life: in t presence is fullness of joy; at thy right hand there are pleasures forever more.

—PSALM 16:11

When my father and mother forsake me, then the Lord will take me up.

—PSALM 27:10

Give unto the Lord Glory due unto his name; worship the Lord in the beauty of holiness.

—PSALM 29:2

The steps of a good man are ordered by the Lord: and he delighteth in his way.

—PSALM 37:23

and

CHAPTER 3 — Part IV
THE FAMILY OF AMRAN: *Al-Imran*
AYAT: 174
It is the devil who only frightens his friends, but fear them not, and fear Me, if you are believers.
(The devil's friends referred to are meant as the hypocrites.)

AYAT: 178
ALLAH will not leave the believers in the condition in which you are until He separates the evil from the good. Nor is ALLAH going to make you acquainted with the unseen, but ALLAH chooses of His Messengers who He pleases. So believe in ALLAH and His Messengers. And if you believe and keep your duty, you will have a great reward.

✝ ✡ ☪ ☯

VERSE:

And fear not them which kill the body, but are not able to kill the soul: but rather fear him which is able to destroy both soul and body in hell.

—MATTHEW 10:28

Let us hear the conclusion of the whole matter: Fear God, and keep his commandments; for this is the whole duty of man.

—ECCLESIASTES 12:13

Ye shall walk after the Lord your God, and fear him, and keep his commandments, and obey his voice, and ye shall serve him, and cleave unto him.

—DEUTERONOMY 13:4

Hearken, my beloved brethren, Hath not God chosen the poor of this world rich in faith, and heirs of the kingdom which he hath promised to them that love him?

—JAMES 2:5

But ye are a chosen generation, a royal priesthood, an holy nation, a peculiar people; that ye should shew forth the praises of him who hath called you out of darkness into his marvelous light:

—1 PETER 2:9

I had fainted, unless I had believed to see the goodness of the Lord in the land of the living.

—PSALM 27:13

For ye have need of patience, that after ye have done the will of God, ye might receive the promise.

—HEBREWS 10: 36

But without faith it is impossible to please him: for he that cometh to God must believe that he is, and that he is a rewarder of them that diligently seek him.

—HEBREWS 11:6

THOUGHT:

In order for one to call oneself a Christian, one must seek and live the attributes of Christ. If you are not doing this, but you are still praising God and worshiping God, you can be a follower of any other religious faith known to mankind. The point to sharing my family's faith in Allah/God, is to evoke thought and change. Not change of religious faith but for us as Christians to challenge ourselves, to see if we were going to be accepting of others' free choice of thinking, living and spirituality. The last time I checked, God gave us all a free choice. We are living in a time where we need spiritual leadership and not RELIGIOUS leadership. If we all walked in love, no matter what religion we practiced, this world would be a better place. I find in Christianity division amongst the faith. One sect believing they are more privileged than another, i.e., Catholic, Baptist, Protestant, COGIC, Holiness, Pentecostal, Episcopalian, etc. I personally pray that I am only sharing God's word to bring people closer to Him, that my walk with Him brings another soul that much closer to seeking and

finding the Lord for themselves. We must begin to love unconditionally and act accordingly toward one another and others. Just
as our personality differences are shared with one another, so is
the Word of God, as you know it, study it and practice it. But many
of us are living in contempt of others for their choices and their
beliefs. That is not our battle; that battle belongs to the Lord.
And to be quite honest, it's not a battle for Him either. We are to
share the word, not debate the Word. The Word is not meant to
be debated. The Word came in the manifestation of man that we
might know what is expected of us while we are on earth enjoying
the gift that God gave to us, His only begotten Son, so that we
may live. The Word is to be shared via behaviors, deeds, works,
love, patience, kindness—verbally, spiritually and emotionally.
God is not a forceful God; He said draw nigh unto Him and He
will draw nigh unto you. He said that if He be lifted up, He would
draw ALL men to Him. This means if you come to Him, He will
surely be there, ready, willing and able. God is a gentleman. He
knows the true meaning of courtship, relationship, then marriage.
Christ did not walk the earth in judgment of people. He desired
that we all see the Father. He prayed for everyone, no matter
their circumstances or beliefs. People to whom we would put our
noses up in the air, Jesus loved, healed, delivered and prayed for
them. People we just would not tolerate because they are not like
us, God loves them.

We send out and receive warm emails about stories that touch
our hearts, as the woman in McDonald's with her husband and
son, and the two homeless men came in and ordered all that they
could afford, a cup of coffee, in order to keep warm. The lady was
unfazed by their smell, but the Christ in her did not allow her to
smell them as everyone in the restaurant did. She in turn ordered
them two meals. She wasn't looking for acceptance from the men

or from the other patrons. She did as Christ would do. She saw a need and filled it. It wasn't about their religious faith or if they had faith at all. It was about her faith and what is expected of her as a child of God, a believer. Her religious faith was never discussed in the email, but those of us who are children of God and have an ounce of spirituality can clearly see that the move and spirit of God was in her. We must all be willing to care for one another mentally, emotionally, spiritually, at times when possible, physically and financially for those of us who are more fortunate than others. This is the Christ that I serve. This is the Christian I desire to be, and pray that I am. I don't want to live my life in judgment of what others do (whether they be Christians or not), how they live, how or who they worship if different than me. I can only pray that the God of my soul is magnified, glorified and lifted up in all the earth. Please note and understand that I am not talking about religious faith that is following man, but faith that follows God's Spirit in us. I believe with ALL of our differences that we will meet again in the heavens above. Because I hold on to what the Word that I serve says. Be blessed and I pray the scriptures and Quranic ayats that have been shared bring about a change in our thought and behavior process toward our fellow man. We can't expect God to accept us as we are, if we are not willing and able to accept others as they are, no matter how different they may be or believe.

PRAYER:

Let the words of my mouth, and the meditation of my heart, be acceptable in thy sight, O Lord, my strength, and my redeemer. Father God, I come to You in these final days to say thank You. Thank You, for free choice. Thank You, for being able to speak, write, teach and glorify Your Word, Lord. I pray that what I have shared with Your people has brought You joy and glory. Father, I thank You for my Muslim family and upbringing for always leading me to be the best Christian I can be, for always being accepting of me and receptive of all the prayers that I send to them, in the name of Jesus. They could be as most Christians do and not receive anything that comes out of my mouth, but they do, Lord, with open arms, hearts and minds. I thank You, for love. Love I have been able to show to others and love I have been able to receive in return. Dear Lord, I pray that Your people experience unconditional love and acceptance in a mighty way for the years to come. I know You are on Your way for Your great return and I pray that all on this prayer list and all that they share Your WORD with, get caught up in the day or hour of Your coming. I thank You for life, peace, health, prosperity, for the brokenhearted, marriage, for being a God of a second chance, for salvation, for the blood of the Lamb, for the homeless, for the lost, for the newly found and for those in service for You. Father, I pray for the safety of our troops. I pray for our government and spiritual leaders. I thank You for guidance and wisdom. I thank You for Your Holy Spirit, for showing me what You would have me to do in these last days. I thank You for letting me see past one year after my first surgery to eradicate my body of cancer. Lord, I love you for MY LIFE and all of those who have conquered this deadly disease, before and after me. Lord, I thank You for the complete healing of my body, for keeping my mind, for keeping me happy, for making a way out of no way, for my job, for my gifts/talents, and for my LOVING family of all faiths. I thank You for showing me early on, what it is to be a friend who loves at ALL times, not when it's convenient, not when things are all good, but a friend NO matter what. Thank You for teaching me and showing me in Your Word that I would have friends that would stick closer to me than a brother. I thank You that my family and friends stick close to me, as well as each other. Father God, I thank You for every soul who has entrusted their children in my care; this has meant the world to a childless mother. But You have made me feel like a mother to many and I appreciate it. I pray that all who receive these verses, my thoughts and this prayer, receive it with the love and honesty it was sent with. Lord, I thank You for being my King of Kings and my Lord of Lords. Thank You, Jesus, for blessing me. I hold steadfast to ALL of the promises that You have made to me and with that said, I thank You, for you're NOT done with me yet. In Jesus' precious Holy name, I pray. Amen! Peace, Nise

✝ ✡ ☪ ☯

Hey family,

What a way to begin the day, resting on what God has done for you in the previous moments and what he will continue to do for you in the moments/days/years to come. You don't need a new resolution for the day or year, ALL you need is GOD!

God Has Kept Me Here For A Reason.

Repeat after me: God has kept me here for a reason. I survived because He has a plan for me. All of your bad relationships, the addictions, the consequences, the bad credit, the repossessions, death of loved ones, the backstabbing from friends, the negative thoughts, or the lack of support; you made it because you are blessed! I release and let go of all past hurts, misunderstandings and grudges because I am abundantly blessed! I recognize them as the illusions they are, and sent from the enemy to kill my spirit, steal my joy, and destroy my faith; For God is all there is. All else is a lie! Now give yourself a hug, wipe your tears away and walk in victory!!!!!!! I love you, but more appropriately, God loves you BEST! Be blessed and know that you are at one with THE SPIRIT OF THE LIVING GOD! And may the Lord keep watch between you and me when we are away from each other. —(Genesis 31:49). Amen!

I trust you will find your reason for being here. Love you all, Peace, Nise

✝ ✡ ☪ ☯

THERE is therefore now no condemnation to them which are in Christ Jesus, who walk not after the flesh, but after the Spirit.

—ROMANS 8:1

THOUGHT:

When you choose and decide to be a follower of Christ, you are not to live a life feeling condemned about past behaviors, attitudes, hurts and lifestyles. You are to live your life in the freedom that God has given you. We are not to be led by man and their rules and regulations. We are not to be walking around giving into all of our little whims; catering to our flesh, continuing to live in the bondage of sin, but led by God's Spirit that He has imparted into us. Understand that God's standards do not change; we are expected to live our lives according to how Christ walked the earth. But, if by chance we do not live God's way or make the mark, His compassion and love don't change; He has unconditional affection and love toward us.

PRAYER:

Father God, I ask that You assist me in keeping Your laws. Help me to live in the freedom of love, peace, grace and mercy that You so lovingly give to me. Lord, You said He who the Son sets free is free indeed; let me begin to walk in that freedom with the knowledge and understanding that in YOU I can do all things. I can live my life in a manner that I am not beating myself up for any and every false move that I make. I desire to walk after the Spirit, after Your Spirit, after the Spirit of Christ. Lord, I thank You for Your loving kindness toward me. Thank You for allowing me to see another day, let alone another year. Thank You for Your Spirit that leads and guides me through my day, through my week, through my life. Holy Father, I ask that You continue to bless Your people and strengthen us to do Your Will and run this race abiding by the blueprint that You sent to us. I ask these things in Jesus' name. Amen.

✝ ✡ ☪ ☯

This book of the law shall not depart out of thy mouth; but thou shalt meditate therein day and night, that thou mayest observe to do according to all that is written therein: for then thou shalt make thy way prosperous, and then thou shalt have good success. Have not I commanded thee? Be strong and of good courage; be not afraid, neither be thou dismayed: for the Lord thy God is with thee whithersoever thou goest.

—JOSHUA 1:8-9

THOUGHT:

God will never leave or forsake you. Meditate on the Word daily, keeping your eyes on God and the letter of His laws will be of ease for you to follow. We will be able to walk upright before Him. We will be able to walk in courage and success over the enemy and his wiles. We will be prosperous in all that we do. Have you ever noticed that when you depart from God's way, not man's way, but God's way that your life seems to fall apart from one end to the other. Don't get me wrong; at times God allows the enemy to take hold of our lives so that He can get the victory over the enemy by our trust, love and faith of our Savior, who is the key to our salvation. God will use your situation as a testimony of your faith, love and trust in Him. At times He allows full deliverance over the enemy and at times He allows us to see it through to the end, still obtaining the victory over the enemy because we did NOT waver in our faith, love or trust in the Father. This is the way to defeat the enemy on every hand. In the process of the attack, we must continue to walk in God's ways. We are commanded NOT to be fearful or dismayed about ANYTHING. Therefore, all that comes your way, God will give you everything that you need to succeed and have the victory. For in God we are more than conquerors, only if we believe. We are VICTORIOUS!!!!!!

PRAYER:

Lord, I want to walk worthy in Your Will for my life. I come to You as an open vessel, ready, willing, and totally available to You. As my favorite song states, "Humbly, I ask thee teach me Your Will, while You are working help me be still. For Satan is busy God is near. Order my steps in Your Word." I thank You for Your love that keeps me through the day. I bask in Your presence. I thank You, for holding my hand when I'm weak and giving me courage to stand. Thank You, for keeping me in perfect peace. Thank You, for Your Word that keeps me every day. Lord, know that I really LOVE You and I pray daily to live in Your will for my life. Father, I ask that You continue to give me the strength, vision, spirit and mindset to share Your Word in love, truth and in peace with Your people. I thank You for the spirit that dwells inside of me. You are the lover of my soul and I thank You. I humble myself to You, knowing that with you there is NOTHING that I cannot do. Lord, I thank You for who I am in You. Thank You for keeping my family covered in Your protective arms. I know without a doubt that Your love abounds ALL ills in this world. I thank You because I know in you, the devil CAN'T have anything that You deem me to have. I rest in the knowledge that what you have for me, it is for me. I believe and receive this in the Mighty name of my Lord and Savior Jesus Christ. Amen.

✝ ✡ ☪ ☯

VERSE:

THE Lord is my shepherd; I shall not want. He maketh me to lie down in green pastures: he leadeth me beside the still waters. He restoreth my soul: he leadeth me in the paths of righteousness for his name's sake. Yea, though I walk through the valley of the shadow of death, I will fear no evil: for thou art with me; thy rod and thy staff they comfort me. Thou preparest a table before me in the presence of mine enemies: thou anointest my head with oil; my cup runneth over. Surely goodness and mercy shall follow me all the days of my life: and I will dwell in the house of the Lord forever.

—PSALM 23

I WAITED patiently for the Lord; and he inclined unto me, and heard my cry. He brought me up also out of a horrible pit, out of the miry clay, and set my foot upon a rock, and established my goings. And he hath put a new song in my mouth, even praise unto our God: many shall see it, and fear, and shall trust in the Lord. Blessed is the man that maketh the Lord his trust, and respecteth not the proud, nor such as turn aside to lies.

—PSALM 40:1-4

I will bless the Lord at all times: his praise shall continually be in my mouth.

—PSALM 34:1

THOUGHT:

Have you ever wondered why Psalm 23 is most people's favorite scripture in the Bible? For me, the scripture is very comforting. I do not fear anything when I put my trust in God. I have found trust allows you a level of comfort others don't have when they go through trials. God will place you in situations with your enemies for you to understand and know for yourself, that He is with you at all times. David knew that with trust, God's grace and mercy will show up for all the appointed days of your life. He further lets us know, that he understood the importance of WAITING on God to make things happen for you; that when you seek the Lord our God, He will incline unto you and hear your prayers, your Victories, your cries, your pain and your sufferings. David lets us know that God can bring you out of the worst situations and sit you in high places where man is baffled as to how you got there. God will establish you on solid, sturdy, unmovable, un-shakable ground, allowing you the ability to STAND still in the midst of the raging storms. It is clear that we are blessed as long as we TRUST God. Because God is the great I AM, we are to be thankful for ALL He has done and will continue to do for us. For merely waking us up in the morning, we ought to praise God with such joy, as we would if our favorite team won a championship. We must continually praise and thank God as He does for us continually on a minute-by-minute, second-by-second, moment-by-moment basis.

PRAYER:

Father God, my heart is full with song and I will sing praises to You with these lyrics, "For every mountain, You've brought me over. For every trial, You've seen me through. For every blessing, Hallelujah. For this I give You praise. You're Jehovah Jirah, You've been my provider. So many times You've met my needs. So many times You've rescued me and I want to thank and praise You." Lord, You have provided for me in ways that I can't understand. I thank You, that because I trust You with my whole heart, I don't even try to understand. I accept my blessings of grace/favor and mercy that You constantly bestow upon me. Thank You for Your Son, David. He keeps me cognizant that, at all times I may, can and will mess up. That I can be a hot livid mess and You will love me anyway. That in my mess, it's OK to seek You, to ask for Your help to get me out of mess. I don't have to hide, run away or turn my back from You because You are an all knowing God who knew me before I was formed in my mother's womb. My Lord who has unconditional love for me, I thank You for the hills and the valleys. There is where You made me. I am proud to be Your daughter and to be able to say that I AM THE BLESSED OF THE LORD. I pray that at the appointed time You will say, "My good and faithful servant, I am well pleased." Thank You for being patient with me. As I continue to wait for You, I surrender to Your leadership, guidance and will to be done. I am standing on Your promises to me, for my life. I praise Your Holy name for You are God alone. You don't need anyone, but we all need You. Thank You for WANTING to be my Father. I love You forever to the end of my time into the beginning of Your time. Bless all that hold You in their hearts and keep to Your commandments. Lord, I will continue to press toward the mark of the high calling in Christ Jesus. In Jesus' name, I pray. Amen.

✝ ✡ ☪ ☯

Praying always with all prayer and supplication in the Spirit, and watching thereunto with all perseverance and supplication for all saints;

—EPHESIANS 6:18

Pray without ceasing.

— 1 THESSALONIANS 5:17

Confess your faults one to another, and pray one for another, that ye may be healed. The effectual fervent prayer of a righteous man availeth much.

—JAMES 5:16

THOUGHT:

As we find in the above scriptures, they speak for themselves. Very self-explanatory, but just in case anyone missed it, we ought to pray. Pray without stopping, pray for yourself, pray for your family, pray for your leaders and pray for one another. Pray earnestly, that what you pray for, you will receive. Pray when you're holy and pray when you're messed up. Pray when it's good and pray when things are going wrong. Live the life of prayer. Pray all of the time. Again, pray not only when you are in trouble. If ever asked, are you your brother's keeper? Well, according to the Word, YES, YOU ARE!

PRAYER:

Lord, the song in my heart for this prayer is that of my Pastor: "I pray for you, you pray for me. I love you, I need you to survive. I won't harm you with words from my mouth. I love you, I need you to survive. You are important to me, I need you to survive." Lord, I thank You for the spirit of being a keeper. I need for all of Your people to survive whatever their lot is. Thank You, for prayer being one of my means of communicating with You. I know I can come to You in many ways and You will hear me. I am glad to be one of your sheep, for You know me when I call You. Lord, thank You for my family. Help them to know the power of prayer and as we accept and pray these prayers together that in our righteousness, our prayers will avail. Let us continue this journey in love, peace, faith and joy, edifying one another according to the will of our Father. Lord, I thank You for the strength to pray without ceasing. I give You all the praise and glory, in the name of Jesus. Amen.

✝ ✡ ☪ ☯

He that is slow to wrath is of great understanding: but he that is hasty of spirit exalteth folly.

—PROVERBS 14:29

A SOFT answer turneth away wrath: but grievous words stir up anger. A man hath joy by the answer of his mouth: and a word spoken in due season, how good is it! The heart of the righteous studieth to answer: but the mouth of the wicked poureth out evil things.

—PROVERBS 15:1 AND 23 AND 28

THOUGHT:

So many times in the Bible, it is pointed out about your MOUTH. The mouth of the just brings forth wisdom. Your mouth/words can speak like piercings of a sword. The words of a tale bearer are as wounds, as they go down into the innermost parts of the belly. There is life and death in the power of the tongue. Even a fool is counted wise when he holds his peace/doesn't speak. The mouth of a righteous man is a well of life. The bottom line is words/things that you say out of your mouth can cause death to you or someone else. When we speak without thinking or in haste, we tend to say the wrong thing at the wrong time, or say the right thing in the wrong way. We need to think before we answer/speak. When you constantly speak evil/negative things, do not get it twisted to think that you are anything other than wicked. We are expected to take these words of wisdom to help keep ourselves out of the mix of talking death into situations and people or our own lives. We are expected to speak life, encouragement, peace, joy, love, acceptance, understanding and legacies of wealth into each other's lives. Not just wealth of finances but wealth of the spirit, wealth of healthy relations, wealth of healthy bodies, wealth of knowledge that will all lead to the success of God's people. Be careful of what you speak and how you speak to your fellow brothers and sisters. We are joint heirs of Christ, making each of us all related by blood, the Blood of the Lamb.

So, if you ever question or have a problem with people who have genuine love of one another and they are not related by DNA but still confess to each other and others that they are family, understand that, the blood relation that I am speaking is a stronger tie than the blood given by our birth or DNA. This blood that I am talking of gave His life that we may live, have life in abundance and be considered as He is to the Father, a child of God. Take it as an honor that this kind of conscious love exists. For some of you, if it had been for the families you come from, you may NEVER know love in its purest form. It is a beautiful thing to know that everyone on MY prayer list I consider to be my family. I have no respect of persons when it is the matter of my heart for the love that I have in my soul toward each and every one of you. I am glad that I was raised to know that not only blood makes you family to another person, but love connects you in the same manner. As when a man marries a woman, they are not blood related, but they instantly become family. The two families merge together forming a larger family. Their children then form the blood bond of family, but it doesn't make them any more or less family than the ones who created them, the mother and the father, the husband

and the wife. Therefore, let's continue to place love at the forefront of our lives to build a stronger larger family that we may continue to build God's Kingdom and destroy all that the enemy has built and continues to build. I pray that I speak life into your lives, souls and spirits yesterday, today and always.

PRAYER:

Father, I pray that everyone that read this prayer understands the power of their words. That they know they can build a life or tear it apart with their words. Father, I ask that You send Your spirit of acceptance and unconditional love to Your children. Not that we only receive it but are able to provide it to others as well. Lord, I ask that You heal the broken. We worship and praise You for all that You are to us. I love You, Lord, and I love who You are in my life. I pray that the words that I speak to people, though they may feel to be harsh at times but necessary and spoken in love, brings forth the best fruit, brings forth growth, brings forth change and brings forth a love of the truth and trust in You. I pray that the words of my mouth are acceptable in YOUR sight. I pray that my light does shine, even in my moments of lack, in my moments of not knowing what to say or how to say it, that I am not nonverbally or verbally speaking anything other than life to Your people. I thank You for Your Word, that I may utilize it as a tool of understanding for my life. I thank You for the personal walk we are having together that others may come to know You as I do. Father, I ask that You perform a physical healing of our bodies, minds and spirits. Lord, touch every doctor, nurse and medical professional that our care is entrusted to. Lord, heal our body, mind and spirit for Your sake, for Your Glory and Your will. That we may live to bring You glory through our life and our children's lives. Lord, bless our family as they encompass around us. Give our children comfort and disband any fears that they may be experiencing. Lead and guide them in any time of the unknown. Let them KNOW that You are the Lord thy God and that You are a constant friend and lover of their souls. Lord, I love Your people as You love us all, with the most unconditional love that I behold. I thank You for leading me to this place of peace, love and acceptance of all Your people. Thank You for keeping me humble and getting me to this place. Thank You for allowing me to see another sunshine of a brand-new day, with brand-new mercy. I thank You for Your goodness, grace and blessings You give to me each and every day. I know through You ALL things are possible. I ask and speak all of these things in the Powerful Mighty Precious Name of Your Son, Jesus Christ. Amen. I love you, Peace, Nise

✝ ✡ ☪ ☯

A double minded man is unstable in all his ways.

—JAMES 1:8

For she said, If I may touch but his clothes, I shall be made whole.

—MARK 5:28

Thou wilt keep him in perfect peace, whose mind is stayed on thee:
because he trusteth in thee.

—ISAIAH 26:3

For as he thinketh in his heart, so is he:...

—PROVERBS 23:7A

THOUGHT:

The power of the mind is a very serious and powerful thing. The saying "mind over matter" comes to my remembrance. What you believe in your mind you will speak or act that thing into existence, whether it's negative or positive. As a nurse of twenty-plus years, I have seen people will life and death into themselves. People that in man's eyes were on their death beds through our Father in Heaven, proved everyone wrong and lived. They had the mindset that they were going to live at ALL costs and they did just that. I have seen this from the smallest of babies to the oldest of elders. I have seen people that felt in their minds that they had nothing to live for that were perfectly healthy and in a matter of blinking an eye, death came upon them. I empower you with the knowledge that you can truly will/think life or death into existence in your own lives. I pray that your thoughts are thoughts of living this life according to God's Will and destiny for you. The Bible teaches us in several scriptures that if we keep our mind stayed on God, He'll keep us in perfect peace. Thank God, if you have no worries or complaints because you are focused on Him and Kingdom building. Seek after the Lord daily and stand on His word that you will receive the desires of your hearts and what He has promised you. Thank God, for first giving you the thought, placing it in your mind and allowing you the ability and talents to follow through to do His Will. Thank God for giving you purpose of a positive mind and not that of negativity. Know that this walk with the Father is a daily walk and know that it is God that keeps you and your mind on a straight path. Know that if you purpose something in your mind, positive or negative, you are no longer operating in God's Will for you, therefore, you will manifest the thought in the manner in which you are thinking.

If you think you are a failure, guess what; nine times out of ten, you will be. You have purposed in your mind and thought process that you can't do anything else but fail. The affirmed woman made it up in her mind that all she needed to do was to touch the hem of the Savior's garment, that she would be completely healed. This is a mighty powerful thought that gave her an abounding unmovable faith to believe that after eighteen years, she would be healed of her infirmity if she just touched a mere thread of Jesus' garment. She really had to think about how she was going to execute getting close enough to Jesus to make this happen. She purposed her plan in her mind, then she manifested that thought into her faith and spirit; she pressed her way through a mob of people and it was done. More people should have this mindset.

Think of the impossible to man to achieve in your mind, execute your plan to achieve that plan, then manifest your victory through your faith in order to see tangible results. For we know that in Christ, ALL things are possible. Oh, what a mighty nation/world we would become. The worst trick to play on yourself is to make your own self believe that the enemy doesn't exist, that if you are thinking one way one minute and then thinking a totally different thing the next second, you are a stable individual. You are a confused individual and God is not in you. For God is not the author of confusion. God gives us a sound mind to make appropriate life choices that we may live this life according to His Will. If you blow whichever way the wind blows, you need to purpose in your mind and heart to change because this is NOT a character God likes to see in His children. He desires our minds, hearts and bodies to be planted in Him as a deep-rooted tree by the river unchanging or wavering because the conditions around it changes. Know and clearly understand that the MIND is a terrible thing to waste. Let's stop wasting it on negativity and begin to utilize our minds and thoughts to create love, peace and honor amongst God's people.

PRAYER:

Lord, I come to You today asking that You keep my mind. Keep it such, there are only thoughts of You and Your ways and Your will. Keep my thoughts that they bring You all of the glory. Father, I ask that You continue to give me the mindset of Christ. Lord, allow me the mindset to press my way no matter what, to see your face and win this race that I may receive the prize of the high calling of You in Christ Jesus. Lord, show me your plan that I may execute it for Your Will in my life. Thank You for my thoughts are thoughts of praise, worship, love, peace, joy, happiness, under-standing, positivity, Kingdom building and success. Lord, continue to guide my mind and thoughts to be of one accord with You, that I am not double-minded, that I seek and have stability in my life. I thank You for Your love, that allows me to trust you without doubt or fear. Thank You for keeping me in perfect peace when my mind is stayed on you. Lord, allow Your people to realize and know that they are the joint heirs of Christ, that there is nothing but Royalty in the midst of your people. Allow them to have the mindset of the Kings and Queens that they are. Let us walk in the liberty of freedom that You bestowed upon us when we live in truth. Continue to heal minds, bodies and souls that we may continue to do Your Will. Father God, I thank You, that I am not a finished product. Thank You for an harmonious mindset that expresses the multifaceted character of You, Dear Lord. Let what I meditate on be acceptable and pleasing in your sight. I continue to pray for the healing of Your children that are hospitalized. Strengthen their minds and body. Let them know that You are the Lord thy God and that ALL things are possible to them that believe. I ask these things and pray for myself and Your people in the name of my Lord and Savior Jesus Christ. Amen.

✝ ✡ ☪ ☯

VERSE:

There is a way that seemeth right unto a man, but the end thereof are the ways of death.

—PROVERBS 14:12 AND PROVERBS 16:25

For that which I do I allow not; for what I would, that do I not: but what I hate, that do I.

—ROMANS 7:15

Let your light so shine before men, that they may see your good works, and glorify your Father which is in heaven.

—MATTHEW 5:16

THOUGHT:

Perhaps there is a reason the particular scripture in Proverbs is repeated almost back to back. Do you think a point was being made? I pray so. I know that many have experienced doing things your way and saw where that has led you. You felt it was your way or no way, your way or the highway. But when you yielded to the Spirit of God within you, you had a better outcome. You came to terms with the fact the only way is God's way. Yeah, we'd like to believe that our way is right until the most horrible end occurs as a result of it. But when GOD says and does something in your life, you realize it was truly the only way to go.

Now, I know the word "death" is a strong word for the writer to use, but I believe that when we continue in our own ways, we physically, mentally, emotionally live a slow and, even in some cases, an instantaneous death. Our spirit toward our heavenly Father dies. We can't hear from God when we are so deep into ourselves. When we don't feed our spirit, we make poor choices that often lead to death. I also believe the writer used the word "death" because as humans, we don't really move to do what is right unless our lives are challenged by death.

Most people know they should live healthy lives by eating right, exercising, avoiding stress and getting proper rest. But most people lead reckless lives, chasing the "American Dream" instead of chasing God's will for their lives. In their quest to achieve the "American Dream," they neglect their own health, working long productive hours for their companies and not living productive lives for themselves, their family or God. In the process they may or may not eat. They eat out more, eating fatty foods, foods high in calories, salt and cholesterol or eating foods prepared in not always the cleanest of conditions. Only you know, when preparing foods, if you are the preparer, whether or not hands are being washed and washed properly. The likelihood that you are achieving proper rest is also in question because you are up early to get to work early and you leave work late to fulfill the obligations of the chase. And for those of you who have families, that have to spend some time with them, it is very taxing on your bodies. No wonder the heart attack, obesity, diabetes, depression, high blood pressure and stroke rates don't decline on a daily basis. With all of the information available to help in the decline of these conditions, people continue to live lifestyles that are not conducive for wellness. People are so eager to live for the dollar not realizing the dollar doesn't care about them. But what and who we should be living for does care a lot about us.

It is written that if we set our affections on above, if we seek God and His Kingdom, all that we live in search and work for will be added unto us. That we'd receive the fullness of God, that God will supply all of our needs according to his riches in glory by Christ. When you walk and work to please God, it feels different than when you walk and work to please man. I know the latter to be the most difficult thing. One, because in pleasing God, I only have to worry about pleasing Him, but if I lived my life pleasing man, even including myself, it would be a mess. There are so many people in my life whom I love dearly and if I lived my life trying to please each and every one of you, surely I would die. Mainly of exhaustion or I'd die from stress. It is a difficult and impossible task to please everyone, especially at the same time. When I please God, He makes me happy. When I please man, this doesn't necessarily make me happy. We are also instructed in the Word to be a pleaser of God and not man pleasers. Check your behaviors and the motive behind your behaviors. Ask yourself, what am I doing and why am I doing it? Also recognize, there are times that you purpose in your heart to do one thing, but you end up doing something else. You try to do right, but you find yourself doing wrong anyway. You know you don't even like doing that thing, you make attempts to change and not do it, but you end up doing it any way. This way of living can also lead to death.

Though God knows this is the nature of some of us, He provides His grace and mercy to see us through it. He wants us to get it together. But He also lets us know that we can't stay in the mud. At some point you need to do what you must do to get out of the mud, especially, when you know to do better. It's one thing if you don't have the knowledge or tools to get out of the mud. But once you gain knowledge and begin to obtain the tools necessary to get out of the mud, you are expected to get out. Do not wallow in the mud when you don't have to. Free yourself from the filth that is in you, that is around you and in your life. If you live your life according to God's laws, you should come across in a manner that attracts people to you and to Christ/the Father. The scripture let your light so shine before men that people will recognize the good that you do and that's in you. Know that it's for God's glory. You are just a player in the game. You are not the main attraction, the God in you is. Family, we must monitor our behaviors and how we come across to others. When we say we love God and we live for Him, our lives should reflect all that God provides us. We should behave in ways that people want to be like us and obtain what we have gained in God. For in God, I lack NOTHING and gain everything, even eternal life. If you begin to seek God and live in His ways, you will see how things begin to change for you.

PRAYER:

Lord, help me to live a life in Your Will filled with love, peace, happiness, joy and success, that others desire to know You because of how I live my life. Lord, forgive me for the things that I say or do, that I really don't want to do but find myself doing anyway. Help me to lead a life of stability. Help me to live in Your perfect Will and not in my own way, because I know my way will lead to destruction and death. Lord, I thank You for grace, mercy and favor. Thank You for loving me even when I fall. Lord, continue to guide me to Your Will/way for me. Thank You for being a Father who supplies ALL of my needs. Lord, as I seek You daily, I pray for Your presence and character in my life. Through Jesus, I pray. Amen.

✝ ✡ ☪ ☯

VERSE:

What? know ye not that your body is the temple of the Holy Ghost which is in you, which ye have of God, and ye are not your own? For ye are bought with a price: therefore glorify God in your body, and in your spirit, which are God's.

— I CORINTHIANS 6:19-20

THOUGHT:

As the scripture states, our bodies are not our own. We must take care of it as a living sacrifice to God for the God in us. We must feed the natural body good nutrition as well as the spiritual body good nutrition. We are taught via the Word that man cannot live on bread alone but by every word that proceeds out of the mouth of the Lord. This is stated at least twice in the Bible. Feeding ourselves the Word gives us the spiritual food needed to live in God and in the world. We are to feed ourselves naturally with a healthy diet and to feed ourselves spiritually with a healthy diet. This keeps us in perfect balance with God. As righteous people we must understand that things will come against us that cause harm to our bodies, minds, souls and spirits. It is up to us to know that it is the trick of the enemy to make us believe God isn't on the throne in charge of everything. You may become afflicted in one form or the other, but God will deliver you out of every last one. The following two scriptures let us know that God is a healer of it all.

But he was wounded for our transgressions, he was bruised for our iniquities: the chastisement of our peace was upon him; and with his stripes we are healed.

—ISAIAH 53:5

and

Who forgiveth all thine iniquities; who healeth all thy diseases;

—PSALM 103:3

A lot of times people only take this to believe it's only for the physical illnesses. Mental illness and spiritual illness is as deadly as they come. I can remember a time when I did not have the Lord in my life as I do now and I had bouts of depressive behaviors. My mind was being attacked and I didn't realize it. The enemy was trying to get rid of the anointing inside of me, so that the day of me sharing God's word to a massive amount of people on a daily basis would not occur. I didn't know that I wasn't feeding my mind the right food. A diet of peace, love, hope and victory, but I fed myself a diet of despair, anger, hurt, pain, failure, hopelessness and death. Maybe I am the only person who did this prior to knowing Whom I belong to and that my body, mind nor spirit was that of my own. I was glad to know that I was healed of any hurt, pain, disappointment, illness, or lack that I was feeling. We should all be glad of a Savior that gives us hope of VICTORY over everything, even death.

PRAYER:

Lord, thank You for being a patient loving God during my times of rebellion to the hearkening of Your call. Thank You for making me realize, that this body in the flesh, mind and spirit is of You. That I am to love me as You love me. For You loved me so much, You gave me Your Son that I may live. Thank You for feeding me Your Word that I may live and share it with others. Thank You, for Your Word sustains me with the most nutritious diet I could ever digest. Father, I thank You for peace, healing, and the spirit that dwells inside of me. Father, I ask that You continue to reveal to Your people their purpose in You that we must maintain health in order to do Your Will in our lives. In order to know what that will is we must continue to feed our minds, souls and spirit Your Word. Lord, we come to You seeking strength, love and knowledge to endure whatever the enemy plans to throw at us to destroy us. Thank You, for we are more than conquerors in Christ Jesus, I pray. Amen.

✝ ✡ ☾★ ☯

VERSE:

For God has not given us the spirit of fear; but of power, and love, and of a sound mind.

—2 TIMOTHY 1:7

For as many are led by the Spirit of God, they are the sons of God.

—ROMANS 8:14

Then he answered and spake unto me, saying, This is the word of the Lord unto Zerrubbabel, saying, Not by my might, nor by power, but by my spirit, saith the Lord of hosts.

—ZECHARIAH 4:6

THOUGHT:

God clearly lets us know that it is not by anything that we possess other than His Spirit that dwells in us that allows us to walk this life. It's by His grace that he provides His Holy Spirit to be our fence, fortress, our mind keeper, our strength, our courage to prevent fear, our all and all. Don't fool yourself into believing that you are doing ANYTHING on your own accord. If it had not been for the Lord who is on my side, I do not have a clue where I would be. When I look back over my life and I begin to see God's work that has occurred, I know He has brought me a mighty long way. God delivers by the power of His Spirit. I believe we struggle in the body of Christ because we have it twisted that it's something that we did to make a situation go a certain way, especially, if the situation turns out in our favor. So let me untwist your thought process and inform you here and now, God is a God of order. He has set a predestined, predetermined time to bring to pass His promise in our lives. But we must first yield to His spirit. Family, have a sweet comfort of knowing that we have an appointment with destiny, with deliverance, with victory and with the Father. It will all be a direct result of the presence of God in our lives. I rest in this assurance of my Father, that He has included me in His plans. I have experienced the reprogramming of my mind, body and spirit through the Word of God. I know that what I speak out of my mouth can affect my mind, thus affects my behavior thus affects my body, which eventually affects my spirit. If you were privileged and took the time to read the scriptures, thoughts and prayers presented to you, you will see that I covered the whole man. God is concerned with the whole body of Christ. Therefore, He is concerned with the whole body of man, which is you, which is me. We are to grow together as a Holy Temple in the Lord through His Spirit in us.

PRAYER:

Lord, as I conclude these entries of verses, thoughts and prayers to remind us that we are the whole body of Christ, and we are to operate as a whole; placing our mouths, minds, behaviors, bodies, health, and spirits under Your subjection in order to do Your Will. Lord, I thank you for your Word, as it leads and guides me every day. I appreciate the anointing that You have placed in me. I know that You would not have entered unless I had invited/welcomed You because You are a gentleman. You don't force yourself on no man. I thank You for the Leaders that You have placed in my life, the late Bishop Barnett K. Thoroughgood and Bishop Hezekiah Walker and my personal spiritual Pastor, Elder Harris. They have helped me attain a closer walk with You, as their delivery of Your word was never forceful but thought-provoking. It left me thirsty, wanting the more of You. They taught me the Bible, the importance of tithing and giving, but most importantly, they taught me that this walk with You is personal, that I am not perfect and that even in You, I will fall but that I must worship You in spirit and in truth. This helped me come to You with my whole self, ready to be an open vessel to be used for Your glory. Thank You, for showing me that walking in the spirit is far better than walking in the flesh, lusting after my own desires for my own pleasure. Now, I thirst for Your Word that has led my desires to be that of what You desire and will for me to have. It is a marvelous feeling that fills me with such love, peace, joy and happiness. Father God, thank You for Your Holy Spirit that dwells in me. It gives me the courage, power, understanding, discernment and love to walk this walk. Lord, I continue to ask You to help me as I walk in the Spirit, that I no longer lust after the flesh, but I have fallen to my flesh. Forgive me when I don't say what is needed to be said, when I say something the wrong way, when I don't act like I know You with my behavior. I know it all to be a sin and I repent and ask Your forgiveness. I thank You for a renewed mind and spirit in You. Father, I ask that all who are under the subjection of this prayer know and understand they are Your children and in You they can live the lives they are seeking. Grant them peace, grace, favor and success on their jobs, in their homes and in their relationships, for Your glory. Let them not operate in pieces but as a whole body. I ask all of these blessings and requests in the name of Jesus my Lord and Savior, I give You all the honor, glory and praise. Amen.

✝ ✡ ☪ ☯

VERSE:

If we confess our sins, he is faithful and just to forgive us our sins, and to cleanse us from all unrighteousness.

—1 John 1:9

And forgive us our sins, for we also forgive every one that is indebted to us. And lead us not into temptation; but deliver us from evil.

—Luke 11:4 (& Matthew 6:12)

Judge not, and ye shall not be judged: condemn not, and ye shall not be condemned: forgive and ye shall be forgiven.

—Luke 6:37

Then said Jesus, Father, forgive them; for they know not what they do.

—Luke 23:34a

But if ye do not forgive, neither will your Father which is in heaven forgive you your trespasses.

—Mark 11:26

THOUGHT:

I have provided several scriptures today and trust there is more I could have shared with you dealing with forgiveness. This goes to show that forgiveness is a tall order. It's something we receive on a daily basis from God through His love, grace and mercy toward us. Forgiveness happens to be the manifestation of your faith. It is the ability to pardon someone who has wronged you. It is the ability to show mercy toward another when they hurt you. Trust, we are truly loved by the Father, especially since some of us have been pardoned from some serious sin. Not that God rates sin, but we know some things are more damaging than others. Forgiveness allows you to have faith in the love you have for a person who hurt you. Faith for the amount of peace you want in your life and faith that God will take care of the situation for you. As we see in scripture, we are commanded to forgive. We are to forgive as God so freely forgives us. I believe we recite the Lord's Prayer without acknowledging our responsibility to forgive. Note, there are times people do things to us and they are unaware that they have wronged us. Better yet, there are times that we may say or do something in deed, in thought or verbally that hurts another without us realizing that we did it. All require forgiveness.

Know that it is a sin NOT to forgive. I ask God to forgive me on the regular because I may have offended someone and not even know that I did it. Lack of forgiveness can eat you up spiritually, emotionally and physically. Please realize your destiny is tied to forgiveness. Your destiny and blessing can be delayed because you have no forgiveness in your heart. I decided a while ago that I wasn't going to allow unforgiveness to get in the way of my destiny, my joy, my peace, my happiness or my Savior. I can honestly say that I have forgiven all those whom I believe have wronged me. I make it my personal effort NOT to let the hurt eat me up and consume my present or future. Don't get me wrong; I haven't forgotten the hurt or the people who hurt me. But I do realize dwelling on it takes my energy and daily walk with God away. It made me angry, bitter, violent and just plain evil. I didn't want to live my life that way. I've learned the hard way to let go and let God. I may react for a second or two—all right, maybe a little longer—but it never goes into the next day. I know some of you can benefit from Letting Go and Letting God!!!!

PRAYER:

Lord, I ask that You forgive me and those praying this prayer for anything we may have done in words, thoughts or deeds that may have hurt someone without our knowledge. Lord, place the spirit of forgiveness in our hearts. Lord, don't allow your people to miss the mark in their unforgiveness. Allow Your Word to resonate in our hearts, minds and spirits that we may lead a Christ-like walk in our journey of life. Father, I ask that you release the burden of the inability to forgive in anyone that is currently experiencing this brick wall. Lord, help them to understand that they become defeated when they continue to have such imbalance in their hearts. I ask that You guide them to forgiveness that they don't delay, block or lose their blessings or destiny. Lord, let them not deceive themselves into believing they are better off in a state of bitterness. Give them a vision/clear look at how that trait kills their joy. It may not manifest itself in the manner in which they expect it to. But it will destroy their joy, peace, and happiness nonetheless. Lord, I love You and I pray that Your people love You enough to be obedient to Your Word. Father, I thank You for your grace, mercy, forgiveness and love of me. I ask, these requests in prayer, in the name of Jesus. Amen.

✝ ✡ ☪ ☯

For the battle is not yours, but God's. Ye shall not need to fight in this battle: set yourselves, stand ye still, and see the salvation of the Lord with you, O Judah and Jerusalem: fear not, nor be dismayed; tomorrow go out against them: for the Lord will be with you.

—2 CHRONICLES 20:15B AND 17

The Lord is on my side; I will not fear: what can man do unto me?
—PSALM 118:6

What can we then say to these things? If God be for us, who can be against us?

—ROMANS 8:31

There shall be not any man be able to stand before the all the days of thy life: as I was with Moses, so I will be thee: I will not fail thee, nor forsake thee.

—JOSHUA 1:5

THOUGHT:

Throughout the Bible, it is reiterated in book after book, testimony after testimony, and parable after parable that God will be with us, that we are not alone, and that whatever you are going through, no matter how big or small, God will be right there with you. If we believe the Word to be true, why is it so many of you are living in fear? Fear to have what God has for you, fear of what you want and desire for yourself, fear of the unknown, fear of what others say about you/think about you, fear of success, fear of failure, fear of love, fear of totally letting go, fear, fear, fear. I mean seriously, how are you living? I am glad to be living in the freedom the Lord has provided me. I don't fear anything. I have taken the examples of the Word, the examples of my own life and the examples of others to empower me to be fearless. I don't fear failure because I know if I failed at something, I had the guts, the audacity and the courage to do it in the first place. This in itself makes me a winner and I know in God's eyes, I am a winner. Therefore, all else doesn't matter to me. I know that I am not where I want to be, but most importantly, I know that I am not where I used to be or where God is going to have me at the finish line.

We must understand that God is with us in ALL that we do. He may not be pleased with ALL that we do, but he's right there. Things you think you can handle on your own, you really need to turn it over to God. I know I spoke on let go and let God earlier in regard to forgiveness, but that statement should stand for every dilemma that you have in your life; every aspect of your life that is giving you a difficult time, stop fighting it on your own. You have someone bigger in the rink than any problem will ever be. Stand on God's word that He will never leave nor forsake you, that the battle is not yours; it's the Lord's, that if God is on your side who/what/when should you have fear, that even when a multitude of people, problems or situations come your way, GOD has your back; GOD will handle it. Remove yourself from the equation and see how quick the fight is over. If only one person shows up for the fight, where is the fight? I've never seen a fight with just one person. You must stop showing up to deal with the mess. Keep doing what you know to do. Keep doing what is right to do. Most of us are so accustomed to fighting—maybe I am only talking about myself—that when you know you can walk away and let something go, you don't. We want to fight to the death. And believe me, family, some of us are dying in the fight. You are killing yourself. If you are fighting, you need to stop! If you are fighting to love, stop. If you are fighting to do what's right, stop fighting it and just DO what is right. If you are fighting to stay in a situation/relationship that you know should be over, STOP, and get out. God will handle the debris from the fight. Don't you worry about picking up the pieces; God has all of the pieces. Don't be like Lot's wife and look back and turn into a pile of dust. Looking back/going back like YOU have the authority to change what has been done. Just do you, take care of you, let the other part of your issue be handled by God. Let God do Him. God is God all by himself. He doesn't need our help in ANYTHING; did ya'll hear me? He doesn't need our help, so step aside, continue to pray, walk in love, praise God, and live the life God has ordained you to live.

Understand and know that if anyone, especially a person of the same faith as you, is against anything that you hold dear to your heart, especially your dreams/visions, know today, they are not for you. They are against you. Furthermore, they are not for the God that you serve. Leave fear for those without faith, for those who don't serve a mighty God, for those who place man above God and for those who clearly don't know the God that you know. For my God supplies ALL of my needs according to His riches and glory. My God is Lord of Lord and King of Kings. My God is mighty in battle and has NEVER lost a fight known to man. The God that I serve survived the cross, the crucifixion and His death. There is NO way I don't want him by my side.

PRAYER:

Lord, I come to You to bless You with a heart of thanksgiving. I want to thank You for being on my side, for being with me in times of troubles. Thank You for being with me when I am asleep, for watching over me and protecting me. Thank You for waking me up every day. I want to thank You for the many times You woke me when I wasn't breathing so that I could take the breath I needed in order for me to still be here today. Lord, thank You for walking with me, talking with me, laughing with me, singing to me and dancing with me. Thank You for taking me on trips, sitting there with me when I am on the plane. Thank You for safe travels. Thank You for accompanying me home during those late nights. Thank You for fighting my battles with the enemy; some battles were known and unknown to me. Thank You for keeping me from falling. Thank You for showing yourself to me on many occasions that I have no fears. Thank You for Your love, patience and wisdom. Thank You for letting me know in mind, body and spirit, that You are with me at ALL times. Thank You for the family You have given me; I love them with the love of my heart. Thank You for Your sacrifice on the cross that has given me my future, my children's future and their children's future. I don't doubt that what I have prayed today is anything but truth. I pray this truth, in the name of Jesus Christ. Amen.

✝ ✡ ☪ ☯

There hath no temptation taken you but such as is common to man: but God is faithful, who will not suffer you to be tempted above that ye are able; but will with the temptation also make a way to escape, that ye may be able to bear it.

— I CORINTHIANS 10:13

My son, if sinners entice thee, consent thou not. My son, walk not thou in the way with them; refrain thy foot from their path. Because I have called, and ye refused; I have stretched out my hand, and no man regarded;

—PROVERBS 1:10, 15 AND 24

THOUGHT:

This is going to be very liberating. GOD has made a way for you to escape ANY temptation/situation that is put before you. Temptation is about YOUR will. It moves for what you want to do even though you know it's not what you are supposed to do. You desire to do right, but you war with your flesh/what you want to do and it keeps you doing what is contrary to God. Be mindful that you can't be tempted with something that you are not attracted to, that you don't like or don't want. Temptation is a test of the enemy. The enemy brings the test to see if he has the power over you. If your response falls victim to what he wants you to do and not what God said to do, he knows that he has you where he wants you. Fight the temptation in the spirit and go to and through the battleground in faith. God fights your battles for you when you have enough faith to go through the battle. When you fight in the flesh, you will fall victim to the enemy. Though some things and people you have attached yourself to, you are going to have to fight to get out of it. If you don't fight it, it will stay in you. Be honest about your struggle/what you're being tempted in. If you're being enticed, don't fall into it. Confront what you need to confront. Face the fact that the relationship you are in is over. Confront the fact that the person YOU picked is not for you. Confront the fact that you married the wrong person. Face the fact you're NOT living the life God has predestined you to be living. These are some of the primary reasons we deal with stress because we are in situations or relationships God did NOT ordain. Fight for your freedom, fight for your deliverance. Utilize the Holy Spirit to help you fight the temptation, to help you get your joy and peace back. Stop trying to hold on to things/people God NEVER intended you to have or be with. My mom used to say, what may feel good to you may not be good for you.

The Word teaches and instructs us how to live right, walk right and how to avoid trouble/temptations before they ever come. But if and when they come, you should know God makes a way for you to get out of it/to escape it. Accept that you've made the wrong choice, correct it and move on in God. Temptations come when the enemy is trying to stop your destiny, when you are try-ing to change your way of life for the better, to deviate you from your path, and make you get out of line with God. The Word has already let you know that what the enemy means for your bad, God will turn it around for your good. When you operate in a compromising environment, know that it makes it harder for you to escape the temptation. DON'T go over to a person's house late if you KNOW you are attracted to them and you KNOW having a relationship, especially sexual relationship, is not what you want. Because when you get there, guess who is having SEX! God gave you a way to escape this by giving you enough time in between to say no and to turn your car around. Sometimes it will be traffic, it can be an accident, the train had troubles; it can be anything and instead of you NOT going to your destination of the temptation, you press your way to the temptation and then be upset with God for not stopping YOU. Well, with all the obstacles placed before you and you don't take heed to them, you take the power out of God's hands/will and place them in your own hands/ your will.

Understand God will give you the desires of your heart. He is not a liar, and though it is not what He wants for you, because He is your Father, He allows you to have it. In reality the only person you need to be upset with is yourself. Because you deceived yourself into believing YOU had the power to get out of a situation, you know in your heart of hearts, you wanted in the first place. Always look for your way to escape a situation or a temptation. Trust a way is always there; open the door and go through it. Whether you are ready or not, take the way of escape God has placed before you. Because He who the Son sets free is free indeed.

PRAYER:

Father God, I ask that You help me as I may have ruffled some feathers, even my own. I ask for the strength, courage and wisdom to deal with ANYTHING that is contrary to You in my life. Lord, I ask that You remove anything or anyone in my life that will weaken the spirit You have placed inside of me. Allow me to know my limitations and to operate in the power You have given me. I ask that You continue to reveal the door to me that I may escape anything contrary to You that comes my way. I ask for deliverance of Your people that are in bondage. Lord, I thank You for the way of escape. Thank You for being ever present, guiding me, being a lamp unto my feet, and keeping me from falling. Lord, I ask that if I fall, that the lesson is learned and that it is for Your glory. For it is at those times the enemy thinks he has me. I thank You for the spirit to persevere, survive, conquer and win. I thank You for all victories past, present and future. Thank You for all the battles I fought, won and loss but learned and taught my joint heirs that they will be able to conquer. Lord, I thank You, because I am free today. I love You, Lord, and I lift my voice to worship You with all my soul. Lord, bless those praying this prayer. I pray and ask these things of You, Father, in the mighty name of Jesus. Amen.

✝ ✡ ☪ ☯

STAND fast therefore in the liberty where-with Christ hath made us free, and be not entangled with the yoke of bondage.

—GALATIANS 5:1

Bear ye one another's burdens, and so fulfill the law of Christ.

—GALATIANS 6:2

Before I formed thee in the belly I knew thee; and before thou camest forth out of the womb I sanctified thee, and ordained thee a prophet unto the nations.

—JEREMIAH 1:5

THOUGHT:

I don't know of anyone with a past who hasn't been able to come to the Lord. Look at Rahab (she was a harlot), Mary Magdalene (she was a prostitute), David (he was an adulterer and murderer), and Tamar (was raped by her brother and tossed away to be made to feel worthless). These were just a few who had a past that was tainted, but believe me, ALL were used mightily by God and not condemned for their past. Therefore, if God doesn't condemn us for our past, how is it we are easily ready to judge the next person for their past or better yet judge ourselves? You must understand that the chains that bind you, often come from events that you have no control over and sometimes come because you willfully live a life that brings about bondage and pain. Regardless of the cause or source of the bondage, get it in your minds, hearts and spirits that Jesus came to free you. God heals, forgives and restores you to who He ordained you to be from the beginning. Prior to you being born or ever being thought of being born, God knew exactly who you would be, how you would act, and where you would be at this exact moment in your life.

Realize you are not in this thing alone; God is always there and we are instructed to bear each other's burdens. This doesn't mean because someone is suffering we must suffer with them. It does, however, mean that we need to help ease their burden to the best of our ability. This means that we are to provide each other with at minimum, compassion, love, empathy, knowledge, counsel and understanding that we all have had some type of way we are/were bound. Sometimes this is all a person needs to feel the relief of the burdens they are carrying. Whether it's the burden of our past, poor decisions made, fear of success, failing, being happy and yes, believe it or not, some people are afraid to be happy. They want to be miserable because it gives them the attention they are craving. We have to be supportive and understand that transformation, change and the desire to actually be freed is a process. A process that isn't always easy and we need others who have been there and done that to assist those to their freedom.

I know it is what Christ did for us, therefore, it is expected of us to do the same for others. I also know that I need patience in this area, because I have a hard time when choices are obvious. Choosing happiness, peace, freedom and love over misery, sadness, bondage and hate. I ask that you all pray for me in this area of my life. Come to terms the fact that God knows the hope and goal of your calling. If you or no one else knows who you are, God knows and God will inevitably show you your real identity. Begin to look for and find the potential of your future because of God's power operating in your life. I truly urge each and every one of you to walk in the freedom God gives to each of us. Your life will turn around immediately!

PRAYER:

Lord, I come to You today strong in my convictions of who YOU say that I am. I stand in the identity that You have given me and I renounce every memory of who I was even up until yesterday. I have come to You in my Father's name. Thank You for anointing my head, counseling my spirit and teaching me who I am. Lord, I thank You that your opinion is ALL that matters to me. Thank You for being my liberator. Lord, I know if no one else knows, You know what it is like to suffer pain and abuse at the hands of others, yet You proclaim joy, peace, love and strength. I claim joy, peace, love and strength for myself. Thank You for the spirit of praise instead of the spirit of heaviness. Lord, loose anyone who is feeling the heavy burdens/spirit of heaviness in their lives, as You have brought me to continue to pray on burdens, and yokes needing to be broken. Lord, I know that I can come to You broken, wounded, hurt, brokenhearted, poor, rich, sick, in need of healing, disgusted, in need of patience, ashamed and bound to be delivered and set free. I declare freedom, joy, peace and happiness NOW in the lives of Your people. Lord, I pray that what I ask be done in the Mighty Name of Jesus until the day of His coming. Amen.

✝ ✡ ☾★ ☯

VERSE:

When I was a child, I spoke as a child, I understood as a child, I thought as a child: but when I became a man, I put away childish things.

— 1 CORINTHIANS 13:11

THOUGHT:

Children walk around blaming everybody for things that they do. They point fingers and say you did it; no, she did it, no, he did it. Everybody but them did the deed. As we grow we learn to take responsibility for our thoughts, for what we say and our actions. When you mature into your grown self, you learn to point your finger at your own self. Recognize your own junk and deal with it. As you mature you should want to move forward with your life. When we go from childhood to adulthood, we are constantly making changes in our lives. Just like you go from stage to stage in childhood, the same holds true in your adult life. And with God you change and go from one level to the next. As every day is a new day, you must grow daily and seek your position in God. When you were a child, you tried to understand everything and constantly asked questions because you "needed" to know. Remember this question, but WHY???? But, when you are an adult and come to the Lord, you begin to know that you won't understand or need to understand everything.

We are taught to trust God and love Him, knowing that He is

going to change you to deal with your situation and growth process. If you notice, He doesn't change your situation; God changes you in order to handle the situation. God is developing you. Do you realize attitudes affect the way you live your life? A good attitude can bring success and a poor attitude can bring destruction. I have found that attitudes are a result of our growth process and per-spectives. Depending on how we grow up is how we will perceive a situation and it will determine our attitude about the situation. This is why not too many people share the same perspective. In one situation ten people can be involved and all ten people can have a different perspective about the situation. The differences of the perspectives at hand are due to the way each individual looks at life, their comprehension level and understanding of what is presented to them. The way one looks at life is often determined by your history/past. Your past can cause you to have an outlook/perspective on life that is not in line with God's perspective of your life in Him. Meaning, how you see it, God doesn't see it that way. You may see your life as if you are a failure. But God doesn't see it that way because He knows your end. He knows exactly how your story will end. You are in the middle of the book, He knows you're in the middle and He is doing all He can to ensure that you get to His end. The problem comes when we don't grow the way in which we should. We are trying to hold onto childhood things that should have been left in childhood. Put those things away. Know that they came about to ultimately lead you to God's purpose in you, which is your destiny. Go forward, be a MAN/WOMAN and get what God has for you!

PRAYER:

Early in the morning do I seek you, Lord. Father God, I am grateful for growth, age and wisdom. I thank You for every day that You give me to bring my life closer to the destiny You preordained and predestined me to have. Lord, help Your people put their past where they belong, in the past. Lord, help us to look past our perspective and change our attitudes. I pray for growth in Your people, that they are living the adult life as You would have them to do. Lord, allow Your people to embrace all that their lives bring them and for them not to place blame on anyone else. Lord, help us to become responsible and accountable for our behaviors. Lord, I ask that You bless everyone under the subjection of this prayer. Bless everything that they touch. Bless their homes. Bless their children. Bless their spouses or significant others. Bless their finances. Bless them at their jobs. Bless them with a job if this is what they stand in need of. Bless their comings and their goings in the powerful name of Jesus. Lord, I'd like to thank You for granting each and every one of us with another moment to enjoy our lives and bring our destiny to pass. Lord, grant us the desires of our hearts and free us from ANY and ALL burdens that we may be facing today or in our future. I pray and ask these things in the name of Jesus. Amen.

✝ ✡ ☪ ☯

And the Lord answered me, and said, Write the vision, and make it plain upon the tables, that he may run that readeth it. For the vision is yet for an appointed time, but at the end it shall speak, and not lie: though it tarry, wait for it; because it will surely come, it will not tarry

—HABAKKUK 2:2-3

THOUGHT:

In the very first verse of the first chapter of the book of Habakkuk states the burden which Habakkuk the prophet did see. Sometimes God gives us a vision and as the scripture above reads, He instructs us to write down the vision and make it plain. I believe He tells us to write it down, so that when the vision comes to pass, people can't deny that you knew beforehand what was going to occur and that it was of God. To some this can be a burden. A burden to keep the vision God gave you to yourself in fear of someone not believing in your vision. Fear that someone may steal the vision God has given you or fear that they will sabotage the vision. The funny part to this is there is an appointed time of the vision coming to pass that has NOTHING to do with man but EVERYTHING to do with God. If the vision was given to you/planted inside of you by God, there is NOTHING anyone can do to make that vision theirs. God will ALWAYS get the glory out of His plan for your life. It should be a sweet victory for you to see the vision of what God has for you. No, you may not know the timing of the vision coming to pass, but you should have the faith and joy to know that it will come to pass. Our true struggle is not with the vision; it is in waiting for the appointed time of our destiny/vision to come to pass.

Understand that God is a God of order. He does everything in His time. He has a set predetermined time to bring to pass the promises He has made in our lives. The time is already set up. Through ALL of the storms, trials and tribulations that we go through, God has already made a way of escape for you just so your destiny can be fulfilled. We should gain and possess comfort in knowing that we all have a God designated appointment with destiny. We should realize that our current situations are temporary and God has a time for our deliverance. Have peace in knowing that NOTHING the enemy does can stop the plan of God in our lives. We must also realize that we can't rush God. God giving us the vision is like us planting seeds and expecting growth right away. Just as it takes time for the seed to grow into what it is expected to grow into. The vision needs cultivating, nurturing, nourishment and growing time in the fertile ground or soil of our faith-filled hearts and minds until we and the vision reach the time of maturation. We have to grow with what was planted inside of us as well.

If you are not open, mature or fertile for growth, it won't happen. The vision will become worthless because it will die before the process begins. Have you ever had a plant that began to outgrow its pot? Nine times out of ten, the plant began to die until you put it in a larger pot. Once we grow, mature, come out of our childish ways and trust God to fulfill the vision, it will come to pass as a direct result of the presence of God in our lives. I take rest in God that what He has placed inside of me, the vision He allowed me to see, it WILL come to pass at His appointed time. I am glad and at peace, that God has included me, as well as ALL of you, in the very intricate details of His plan. I accept and rejoice that what God has for me, IT IS FOR ME!

PRAYER:

Lord, I thank You for peace, knowing that what You have for me is for me and no one else. I thank You that I don't desire anyone else's dream, vision or life except the one You have birthed and ordained me to have. Thank You, Lord, for growth, wisdom, age, knowledge, faith and maturity. Thank You for planting a mighty seed inside of me. I take no credit for it; the glory belongs to You for at your appointed time it has and it will come to pass. I speak those things as though they are when they are not. I trust in Your Word that tells me I can and I have faith larger than a mustard seed that what MY Father said I can have is far greater and more abundant than I could ever imagine, ask for or dream of. Lord, I know in order for Your people to be ready for the vision/seeds planted inside of us, we must go through some unpleasant as well as pleasant times. Lord, keep us humble, let us learn from all that we encounter. Thank You, that we don't choose destiny; it chooses us. Father, I thank You for joy in times of trouble. Thank You for Your Word as a lamp unto my feet. Father, I love You and I will praise Your Holy name for all of the appointed days of my life, in Jesus' name, I pray. Amen.

✝ ✡ ☪ ☯

VERSE:

And behold, there was a woman which had a spirit of infirmity eighteen years, and was bowed together, and could in no wise lift up herself. And when Jesus saw her, he called her to him, and said unto her, Woman, thou art loosed from thine infirmity. And he laid his hands on her: and immediately she was made straight, and glorified God.

—LUKE 13:11-13

THOUGHT:

For a minute God has led me to deal with the issue of BURDENS. Well, it looks like today won't be any different. It is apparent that many of us have things that we need to be separated from or burdens that need to be lifted off of us. People, I pray that you all are hearing me and taking heed to the Word of God, which frees us and gives us comfort, and refuge from our burdens, worries and cares. We will NOT function effectively until those things or burdens are lifted off of us. Don't get me wrong; you can coexist, but the effectiveness of that coexistence will be stifled if you remain under the very thing you need to let loose. Perhaps some of you have things that are burdening/holding you down. If this is the case, you need to commend yourself for being able to carry on thus far under that weighted pressure. Unfortunately, many of us bear the weight of the burden alone, mainly because you don't feel free enough to tell anyone about your struggles. It is God's intention that we be set free from the burdens/loads that we bear and carry.

Even though the Word tells us to bring EVERYTHING to God in prayer, to cast ALL of our cares upon Him and for those who are heavy-laden and burdened, He would give us rest in Him. The bottom line is that we don't stand on God's Word that we can actually do these things. If we truly believed it, you would not be burdened down with anything right now. But I know some of you are. Some of you are living in codependent heavyweight relationships. Others are anesthetized to your problems because they have been going on for so long that you don't even feel the weight of the burden anymore. Some of you have become so accustomed to having a problem, that even when you have the opportunity to be delivered and set free from it, you find it hard to let go of the very thing that is keeping you bound, that is weighing you down and that is burdening you. The burdens become like a security blanket.

In the scripture above, when Jesus said, "Woman thou art loosed from thine infirmity," He took away the woman's excuse to remain sick. For eighteen years she could excuse herself due to her infirmity. But the moment, not two weeks later, not a year later, but IMMEDIATELY when He told her, her problem/situation was gone, she no longer had an excuse nor did she try to make any. She did as Jesus told her to do and she got up and walked in Victory. This is the same thing you all need to understand; when you are in Christ and you profess to love the God that you serve, you minimize who God is by not letting go of something, even if you're afraid to. If God said to let it go, you need to just LET IT GO!!! Give your burdens over to God. He will work it out for you. Family, I charge you to walk in the VICTORY our Lord and Savior has given to us in HIM!

PRAYER:

Father God in Heaven, I pray that all that I put before Your people this week allows for freedom and deliverance. I pray that someone is loosed from the burden(s) that have been weighing them down. Lord, I thank You for deliverance, healing and the liberty of freedom that I gladly walk in. Lord, I trust You with my whole heart. Lord, Your people need you in a mighty way, for they are carrying around things and people in their hearts, minds and souls that they know they need to let go of. They know it's holding them back, but the enemy has tricked them into believing that if they hold on to it long enough, it won't matter and it will go away. Lord, I am standing in the gap for my family in this area, as I know what it was like to be bound by burdens, bills, fears, love of another, loss of my child, anger and a fighting spirit. Thank You for freeing me of each and every one of the things that did not allow me to stand on Your promises. Lord, You state in your Word that people perish from lack of knowledge and I pray I have given them enough Word to assist them to have the knowledge that You are Who You say that You are, that You are a deliverer, comforter, healer, burden carrier, provider, friend, lover of souls, trustworthy and the truth. Lord, I pray that all who need to take heed to your call for them to let the burdens go and be set free will do so. I thank You for covering each and every one of us praying this prayer with the blood of Jesus. And it is in Jesus' name that I pray and ask these things and count them done in the boldness I have been given through Your precious Holy Spirit. Amen.

✝ ✡ ☪ ☯

Remember ye not the former things, neither consider the things of old. Behold, I will do a new thing; now it shall spring forth; shall ye not know it? I will even make a way in the wilderness, and rivers in the desert.

—Isaiah 43:18-19

THOUGHT:

Let go of the old stuff and expect a new thing to happen. Not only are we expected to let the past go, we are instructed to not even REMEMBER the past. Understand that your future starts NOW!!!! Be finished with the old. Talk, think and behave in new ways. Do things differently in order for you to be brought to new levels in God. Make up in your mind to declare new things, regardless of what is going on in your life now and what has happened in your past. God created you to be new in Him. God will make a way for you to change and become new even when it doesn't seem possible. You can be in the worst of conditions, the driest of places and He will make a way for you to make the necessary changes in your life to be what He ordained you to be. Family, NOW is the time for you to become what God wants you to be. God is not concerned with where you come from or where you are at today. He is concerned with where you are going, and trust, in the process, He is developing you and taking you to the next level in Him.

PRAYER:

Father God, I thank You for forming me for Yourself. I thank You for making a way for me, sometimes a way out of NO way. You are a provider, healer, deliverer and potter. Thank You for molding me into who You want me to be. Lord, thank You for teaching me through trials and tribulations that I can one, get over them; two, I don't have to be defined from them; and three, I can let them go and not even remember any of them. Lord, I thank You for doing a new thing in me. I thank You for showing me the ways in which I need to change for with those changes, my life is for the better. Thank You for the joy, peace, happiness and laughter I get in my life. Lord, I understand that my life is not my own. I desire to please You and bring You glory, Lord. Lord, I understand that I can only do what You allow me to do and with this knowledge, I am aware that I can do ALL things through Christ Who strengthens me. Lord, I thank You that in spite of my past, You have called me to a mighty purpose-filled life in You. I love You, I stand on your Word and I praise Your Holy name. I pray in the name of Jesus. Amen.

✝ ✡ ☪ ☯

Cast away from you all your transgressions, whereby ye have transgressed; and make you a new heart and a new spirit: for why will ye die, O house of Israel?

—EZEKIEL 18:31

THOUGHT:

Be conscientious of your sins and repent. This means to turn away/move away from all the sin in your life. This is a conscious act. It requires you to take action and do it willfully. Take responsibility, say you're guilty and change your ways. God WILL change YOU to deal with your situation. He won't change the situation or season; you must go through it. We all know that seasons change and end. The same stands for trouble; it doesn't last always. Holding on to to your past will cause you to not grow and die. If you remotely want to live a happy life, you are going to have to get rid of all things that are not of God. Clear your heart and mind of ill feelings and thoughts. Feed yourself positive thoughts and behaviors and you will begin to see results in your life giving you the VICTORY over your sins/past. It truly is that simple.

PRAYER:

Lord, I seek Your face early in the morning to ask You to create in me a clean heart and renew the right spirit within me. You are my strength and my redeemer. Lord, Your people are in need of change. Father, I ask that You order my steps that will remove any and all sin that exist in my life. Lord, I know I can't do this on my own and I am seeking You in an urgent manner for the releasing of sin and the change of hearts, minds, spirits and behaviors. Lord, I desire to live in the fullness of the joy You have given me. I thank You for peace, love, forgiveness, understanding and newness. Thank You for allowing me to walk in the newness of all the mercies You bestow upon me every day. Father, I ask that You bless all those reading this prayer, renew their minds, bodies, souls, behaviors and spirits. In the name of Jesus, I pray. Amen.

✝ ✡ ☪ ☯

For I will take you from among the heathen, and gather you out of all countries, and will bring you into your own land. Then will I sprinkle clean water upon you, and ye shall be clean: from all your filthiness, and from all your idols, will I cleanse you. A new heart also will I give you, and a new spirit will I put within you: and I will take away the stony heart out of your flesh, and I will give you a heart of flesh. And I will put my spirit within you, and cause you to walk in my statutes, and ye shall keep my judgments, and do them. And ye shall dwell in the land that I gave to your fathers; and ye shall be my people, and I will be your God.

—EZEKIEL 36:24-28

THOUGHT:

God will take you out of all types of situations/circumstances and bring you into a place that is your own. He wants to separate you from things, people and places that are not of Him. When you allow God to clean you up, know that you are clean. There is no question as to whether the process occurred or not. Once God cleans out the dirt on the outside, He begins to work on the inside to your heart and your spirit. When God puts His Spirit inside of you, it causes you to walk in the manner in which God walks. The poignant point is God always lets us know that we have free will to allow His spirit to lead and guide; if we keep His statutes and judgments as well as do them, we will have all God placed before our fathers. We become His when we abide in Him and He abides in us. God has placed a seed of greatness inside of you. It is up to you to allow God to birth it. In order for you to live the greatness, the dream, the vision and the anointing that God placed inside of you, you must be clean and free from filthiness, your past, putting others/things before God, and worshipping anything/anybody other than God.

If you notice, when God says He is going to do something for you, it is written as He WILL. The Word doesn't say He may, He might, He could or He would. It is a definitive statement, that He WILL bring all that He says to pass. Trust that when God cleanses you, it is done! When God says He will give you a new heart and He will put His spirit in you, understand that it is done and there is NOTHING that you can do about it!!!!!!!! Therefore, when you are in a pit, sin or trouble, believe and trust God. Don't be so caught up in your current situation(s) or circumstances that you stop trusting God for the promises He has made to you. Every time you see the words "I will," you are looking at the promises of God and you know we are taught to stand on those promises. Though you go through your Job experience, trust that you can live the dream/vision God has placed inside of you because YOU are the temple of the living God inside of you. I doubt very seriously that you would keep God's house a mess. So, clean up your mess, whether it's in your house, relationships, job, mind, body or spirit. Clean it up, clear it out and allow God's purpose to prevail. Family, start anew, leave the past in the past, and begin to move into your destiny.

PRAYER:

Lord, I find that Your people require a renewal of their minds, hearts and spirits. I thank You for Your goodness and mercy. Thank You for a clean heart and a renewed spirit of You within me. I am standing on all of the promises that You have made to me and I WILL be able to see them before the coming of the Lord. Father, I thank You for ALL You have already done for me and if You don't do another thing for me, I praise You, honor You, and love You. Thank You, Jesus, for blessing me. Thank You for keeping me encouraged and not allowing any harm or danger to come my way. Thank You for Your Word as it acts as a shower cleansing me every day that I read Your Word and seek You. Lord, I pray for those who don't know You as I do. For those who don't take Your "I will/your promises" as their own. Thank You for leading and guiding me into the vision You placed in my spirit. Lord, I pray that I am living in the newness of You. Thank You for my family; may they be blessed beyond what they can ever imagine or dream. In the name of Jesus, I pray. Amen.

✝ ✡ ☪ ☯

That ye put off concerning the former conversation the old man,
which is corrupt according to the deceitful lusts; And be renewed in
the spirit of your mind; And that ye put on the new man, which
after God is created in righteousness and true holiness.

—EPHESIANS 4:22-24

That he might sanctify and cleanse it with the washing of water by
the word,

—EPHESIANS 5:26

THOUGHT:

Notice in this scripture we are instructed to put off former
thoughts, conversations and behaviors of our old self—which is,
who we are prior to coming to Christ. We are never perceived as
being perfect or good; we are always in some state of sin. To put
off, take off, cast away, and forget, are all words that require action
from us. The action God is looking for is that we leave all of who
we were in the past. That we become new in what God created us
for, His righteousness, His holiness, and His glory. When we decide
to take heed to the Word of God and leave those things that literally
and figuratively haunt us in the past, we will experience our minds
and spirits become renewed. I believe renewed is used because it
indicates newness being done over and over. The point is you get

rid of one set of baggage, you live your life some more, you mess up and have to put that in a new set of baggage and get rid of that and become new, yet again. This lets us know that you will renew your mind from the past more than once. You don't just come to the Lord once and everything in your life is all good. You will continue to make mistakes, get hurt, feel depressed, suffer losses, become angry, suffer persecution and live in unforgiveness if you don't change your ways, put on the new man in Christ and renew your mind.

Know that in all that you do, good, bad and indifferent, God will sanctify and cleanse you by His Word. The Word of God causes you to clean up your life and it washes all the impurities out of your life. You must understand that every aspect of your life has been conformed by this world and now you must be transformed in God. Transformation doesn't come from inspiration; it takes place in the mind. According to the Bible, we must be transformed through the mind. The struggle we have inside of us is with self-perception. Our perception is affected by those around us, by what they say and do to us, be it positive or negative. It is also affected by being neglected or ignored because it causes our self-worth to be diminished or destroyed. When we come to God, we must grow and walk in our own self-image and not of that being watered down/diluted by the contribution of others. As the body of Christ, we need to progress along with persevering. When you wake up daily, most will change their clothing daily. We do this as a daily process and we need to realize this is something we need to do in our minds. Take out daily what you know needs to be released out of your mind, body and spirit.

PRAYER:

Lord, I thank You for the broken, for if we were not broken, we would not have a need to be fixed. I thank You for the cleansing and renewal of my mind. Thank You for Your Holy Spirit for it is the vessel by which change occurs. Lord, provide Your people with the love of oneself. Cast down any strongholds, especially on the mind, so that Your transformation process can take place on a daily. Father God, we recognize that without You, we would not be able to do anything. Thank You for letting me know that by transforming my mind to think positively, this affects my thoughts which eventually affects what I would say and do and eventually affects the way I live my life. I thank You for ALL of the positive influences in my life. Lord, I ask that You bring Your transforming spirit into Your people such that marriages, health, wealth and mentalities are being transformed. I praise Your Holy name. I thank You for allowing me to see another day in order to grow with the daily transformation of my mind. I pray this prayer with the thought of Your people on my mind and in my heart. I ask these things of You, Lord, in the mighty name of Jesus. Amen.

✝ ✡ ☪ ☯

VERSE:

Behold, I was shapen in iniquity; and in sin did my mother conceive me. Behold, thou desirest truth in the inward parts: and in the hidden part thou shalt make me to know wisdom. Purge me with hyssop, and I shall be clean: wash me, and I shall be whiter than snow. Make me to hear joy and gladness; that the bones which thou hast broken may rejoice. Hide thy face from my sins, and blot out all mine iniquities. Create in me a clean heart, O God; and renew a right spirit within me. Cast me not away from thy presence, and take not thy holy spirit from me. Restore unto me the joy of thy salvation; and uphold me with thy free spirit.

—Psalm 51:5-12

THOUGHT:

And we wonder why David was considered a man after God's own heart. When David said this declaration or prayer, it was after he had been with Bathsheba. Though he sinned and obtained exactly what he wanted, I believe the Holy Spirit convicted him to truly realize that he had sinned. He knew that coveting another man's wife was wrong, but he was so deep in the commitment of satisfying his flesh, he didn't think of it. As soon as he sinned, he acknowledged that he sinned, as we find him here in scripture asking God to forgive him and clean/rid him of the sin committed. We must be as David was; we must always, no matter what it is that we do, recognize the sin that we do, repent and ask God to forgive us, take away the sin and seek restoration from the sin that we committed. To be purged is a deep, inner-cleansing process, as to why he said he will be white as snow. He recognizes that when God gets in the picture to clean him up, he will be pure again. This manner of thinking indicates that David trusted God to get the job done.

By nature we are dysfunctional as people because we are born into sin. We must change our position in life by coming out of sin, then come to the Lord and live a life free from sin. We must understand that we will never be totally free from sin, but we are to live our lives trusting God that we can be free from sin. This way, if we do sin, it's not of a conscious effort. That is why the prayer of asking God to forgive you for things you've done willingly and things you have no clue you may have done, is very important. Know that we commit a sin if another person is offended by a look that we give them, though the look on your part was not meant to offend. You are not even aware that the person even feels in a way about the look you gave them. It doesn't take away from the fact that it's a sin to offend your neighbor/people, according to the Word of God. Knowing this is gaining knowledge/wisdom of God and what is expected of your inner man. If you sin, your spirit should convict you to acknowledge that you did, turn away from such sin and ask for forgiveness for committing that sin. Don't allow NOTHING or NO ONE to come between you and God. Therefore, get up from your current circumstances, live in the new life God has given you via the cleansing of your heart and renewal of your spirit. And walk in the joy God provides in salvation.

Understand that every day is a new day, and if you keep your mind off of yourself and on God, the likelihood of you sinning will be minimal and you will begin to see what is good, acceptable and that of God's perfect will. If you keep thinking about yourself, you will sin along the way. I urge you to keep your mind on

God, ask God to forgive your shortcomings, be encouraged and trust God, that you will be made clean again and walk in righteousness in Him. Family, we must begin to deal with what we are feeding our minds. It is leading folk to all type of sin. I know that in Christ, I am a new creature. I trust that He can do the same for all of us. Allow Him in your hearts, forget about your deep-rooted past and become new again. I love you all and I desire newness for each and every one of you. Be blessed always.

PRAYER:

Lord, I thank You for the heart and spirit of David. Thank You for the encouraging fact that I can have joy in your salvation in spite of my past or current circumstance. Lord, I appreciate every time You have blotted out my transgressions, for I enjoy walking in the newness that You alone give me. Lord, thank You for giving me wisdom on how not to allow any sin that I commit/committed to keep me away from Your loving kindness toward me, from repeating the same sin, and if I find myself repeating the sin, that I can continue to seek You for refuge, forgiveness, strength, love, correction and freedom. Lord, I thank You, that as of today, I am not bound by sin and I am walking in the newness You have given me through Your Holy Spirit. Father God, I pray for Your people as we continue to struggle with the many areas of sin that can be committed. Create in all of us a clean heart and renew a right spirit within us. Oh, Lord, You are my strength and my redeemer. I ask that You bind the devil on every hand. Release the blessings that You so freely give. Father, I ask that You keep those encouraged who may be going through at this moment. Though we have trials and tribulations on every hand, we reach toward You for love and guidance to walk upright in You. Lord, I trust You and I ask these things and many more in the precious name of my Lord and Savior Jesus Christ and I count them ALL done. Amen.

✝ ✡ ☾ ☯

VERSE:

No weapon that is formed against thee shall prosper; and every tongue that shall rise against thee in judgment thou shalt condemn. This is the heritage of the servants of the Lord, and their righteousness is of me, saith the Lord.

—Isaiah 54:17

THOUGHT:

Have you ever noticed that when you feel you are at your best, here comes something/someone attempting to destroy your joy, peace, happiness, success and prosperity? For those of us serving the Lord, do you notice that when all HELL appears to break loose, you are still standing and are intact? This is not luck, good fortune or due to anything that you feel you may have done to prevent the destruction. It has EVERYTHING to do with God's grace, mercy and favor in your life. No matter what the enemy conjures up against you, it won't work. No brilliant lie will work. No putting a banana in the old tail pipe will work (for the *Beverly Hills Cop* fans). No illness or diagnosis will work. No WEAPON or device will work against you to have the victory over you. All of the trickery attempted to make you fail is predicated on your faith. If you believe the enemy can and will have the victory over you, then guess what, they will. But if you have faith as Shadrach, Meshach and Abednego, you will be in the fire and come out without an ash or scent that you were ever near a fire, let alone in a fire. Their faith caused what the King wanted to happen to them, not to happen because they understood that NO MATTER what was done to them, they believed God for their deliverance and breakthrough, even if it was through their death. All they knew was to trust God and praise Him no matter how bad their circumstances looked.

We need to have that same type of faith to make whatever it is God has for you to come to pass. This will occur through your faith and belief in God's Word and the promises He made to you. It is our birthright to obtain favor, grace and mercy over our lives. Be assured that God knows the fiery path you have to walk through in order to get on the road to accomplishment and victory over all of the enemy's tactics to make you fall and then fail. The enemy would like us to believe that because we fell, we won't get up, brush ourselves off and keep it moving. Know that God knows how to take a mess and turn it into a miracle.

And because I have faith that as of today is beyond my comprehension and I am loving it, I can say with victory, the doctors may call it cancer, but God calls it healed, therefore, I call it what GOD calls it. Be blessed and be a blessing. Family, I love you all and will continue to pray for all of us daily. Thank you, Lord, for LIFE!!!!!!!!!!!!

PRAYER:

Lord, I am taking comfort today in knowing that NOTHING the enemy throws my way will prosper in any way against me. Thank You for not giving me everything that I want, as I find it always isn't what is best for me. Thank You, Lord, for I am walking and living in VICTORY. The enemy thought he had me, but You made sure his tactics failed. Thank You for Your Word. Father, I ask that You bless Your people. Lord, give us what we stand in need of today. Lord, increase our territory. Show us all of our ways, things and people that are not of You that we may rid our lives of it/them today, in the name of Jesus. Lord, I am available to You, use me for Your glory. There is no place that I'd rather be than in Your presence. I thank You for my family.

Satan, I know you are somewhere around lurking to destroy what God has for me, but I WON'T let you tear me down and get the victory. Satan, get thee behind me. I am more than a conqueror in my Lord and Savior. Lord, I pray this prayer and ask these blessings to be done in the mighty name of Jesus. Amen.

✝ ✡ ☪ ☯

Ask, and it shall be given you; seek, and ye shall find; knock and it shall be opened. For every one that asketh receiveth; and he that seeketh findeth; and to him that knocketh it shall be opened.

—MATTHEW 7:7-8

Whatever you're asking God for, make sure it lines up with the Word of God. Bless God for what's yours, even if you don't have it already. Sometimes God has what you asked for and He delays the process of you getting it. Remember that delayed is NOT denial. We are often delayed from obtaining the very things that we ask for because we are not ready for what we asked. It may also be that it's not the right time for what we asked for, even though we are ready. And sometimes the delay is due to the fact God has asked some things of you and you haven't done it yet. You can't expect God to do for you when you are unwilling to do what He asks of you. Begin to operate in your life by doing whatever it is that God asks or says for you to do; just do it. As your faith increases, your requirement for the evidence of what God is asking of you will decrease. You will do what He asks, when He asks, with no question. You should also be grown enough to know what you know and not always expect an answer from God. Don't believe that what you have now is as good as it gets. God has better for you. He saves the best for last. Being that God knows what is going to bring us to a place of seeking Him. He'll cause you to be uncomfortable because when you seek and ask things of God, it releases answers. There are times in our lives when we require more from God and we need a Word from Him. The only way the Word is going to come is if we first ask for it. There is a blessing waiting for us and because it is of God, it is worth attaining.

PRAYER:

Lord, it's me, standing in the need of prayer. I come to You daily seeking Your face for the things I require in my life. Lord, I ask for the desires of my heart to be granted. Most importantly, Father, I ask for Your Will to be done in my life. Because You said it in Your Word, that if I ask, I shall receive, and if I seek it, I will find it, and if I knock at the door, it will be opened unto me. I thank You for Your instructions on how I am to obtain what it is that You have for me. Lord, I need Your help in this walk with You. Lord, lead and guide me along the way. I pray that my steps are ordered by You. I put my hope and trust in You. Thank You for giving me the answers to what I ask of You. Thank You for opening doors for me when I seek a way of exit or entry. I thank You for I have sought You and Your ways and I have found them. Lord, I ask for the complete healing of my body. I ask for favor for Your people on their jobs, in their relationships and for their families. I pray that all who read this prayer learn and know for themselves, that what they ask of our Father, they can have it. Lord, I ask that You grant them the desires of their hearts and that You keep us all from harm and danger in the name of Jesus. Amen.

✝ ✡ ☪ ☯

Therefore, my beloved brethren, be ye steadfast, unmovable, always abounding in the work of the Lord, for as much as ye know that your labour is not in vain in the Lord.

— 1 CORINTHIANS 15:58

Now he which stablisheth us with you in Christ, and hath anointed us is God; Who hath also sealed us, and given the earnest of the Spirit in our hearts. Not for that we have dominion over your faith, but are helpers of your joy: for by faith ye stand.

— 2 CORINTHIANS 1:21, 22 AND 24

If it be so, our God whom we serve is able to deliver us from the burning fiery furnace, and he will deliver us out of thine hand, O king.

—DANIEL 3:17

THOUGHT:

I don't know why and truly I am not really trying to figure it out, but I still have to ask, why is it that people think they can do something to a child of God and get away with it? The Word says touch not my anointed and do my prophet NO harm! I have shared scriptures that support, NO WEAPON FORMED AGAINST ME SHALL PROSPER; it won't work!! That should have been an indication for some folk the type of life I, if not all of us, are going to have.

I guess some people truly don't understand the concept of you reap what you sow. When one is established and firmly rooted in God, NOTHING will be able to cause the person to not trust God or stand on God's Word for their deliverance out of the enemy's hands. Let the enemy know his/her tricks will NEVER win. Not because of anything we can do, other than to have faith. But due to the God that we serve, they will NEVER win. So, let the haters hate. I have found, the more they hate on me, the more God blesses me in ways I would have NEVER EVER imagined. And even if I would have imagined it, it has always been far beyond what I could have imagined. Realize if everything you do is for the Lord, then your labor is not in vain. It is not about being cocky; it's about knowing and experiencing the Word and even better, experiencing and knowing the God that you profess to serve. No matter what the enemy throws your way, God's Word prevails!!!!!!!!!!!

PRAYER:

Lord, help the nonbeliever with their faith and belief in You. Let them know that if You said it, so shall it be. Lord, I thank You that I am a survivor of many sufferings. Thank You, Lord, because even now after ALL I've been through, You have given me the power to rise up again. Thank You, Jesus. Lord, I thank You, as I can't change how people treat me, but I can step over my adversity and walk in the newness You have given me in You. Thank you for restoration and deliverance. I Love You, Lord, and I praise Your Holy name. Thank You for the peace, love, joy, and happiness that I have in my heart, especially today. Thank You, Lord, for being on my side. Great is thy faithfulness toward me. Lord, I would be remiss if I did not thank You for the life and death of my daughter, Nyleve; I thank You because her part of my journey has truly shaped and guided me into Your loving arms where I am deeply rooted in You and Your ways. I count it ALL joy, and I am happy I don't desire it to be any other way. I thank You, for my being in Your Will and for giving me the strength, courage and wisdom to know that I can do ALL things in You Who gives me the strength to do it. Lord, continue to cover Your people in the blood of the Lamb. Lead and guide us to do Your Will and bless each of us in a mighty way. I pray this prayer in the name of my Lord and Savior, Jesus Christ. Amen.

✝ ✡ ☪ ☯

VERSE:

Fight the good fight of faith, lay hold on eternal life, whereunto thou art also called, and hast professed a good profession before many witness.
— 1 TIMOTHY 6:12

The thief cometh not, but for to steal, and to kill, and to destroy: I am come that they might have life, and that they might have it more abundantly.
—JOHN 10:10

Dearly beloved, avenge not yourselves, but rather give place unto wrath: for it is written, Vengeance is mine; I will repay, saith the Lord.
—ROMANS 12:19

THOUGHT:

The suffering of the present time doesn't compare to the glory that's on your way. The trial is to test who you are. Your faith is being tried by the enemy, to see if your relationship with God is authentic or not. Are you only serving the Lord because of what you can get from Him? Or, are you serving Him because He is God, end of the story!? Learn to praise and celebrate God when things aren't going right and when things are going well. God is perfecting you in these times until He can see His face in you. Bless God at all times, be glad that God is in you and enjoy the fact of knowing that when you truly trust and believe God, the enemy CAN'T take away your praise or your joy. Serve God with gladness, joy, power and your anointing for the rest of your life. Remember, God is working out the details in your life so that He can see Himself in you. Hold on to your faith, because the first second you show faith, God is going to bless you.

Understand your purpose in order for your destiny to be birthed. Sow into fertile ground. Family, if we don't get anything else, understand the enemy is NOT after your Church—he is after YOU and YOUR house. He wants you to have conflict in your house ALL the days of your life. He wants your joy, love, peace, happiness, your anointing, your children and your life!!! Don't worry, because if God abides in you and you abide in Him, God becomes your defense. You don't have to defend yourself. When God has delivered you, you do not stop what you are doing to answer your accusers. Continue to bless God and keep it moving because you don't want your attitude to become defensive. You can't afford to do business with moods and attitudes. When you allow this to occur, you become vulnerable to defensiveness, low self-esteem and depression. Please understand that these things are of the enemy. ALWAYS remember, the enemy comes to kill, steal, and destroy you. You must get to the point, where you quit defending yourself or attacking others because at this very point, you will cause the Lord to fight for you.

Therefore, keep the faith; live life in the abundance God pre-destined you to have; don't worry yourself with the enemy because God has your back. God and God alone fights our battles. I don't know about you, but this brings me such a level of comfort as to how I am able to go about living this journey without fears but in total faith and Victory in my Lord and Savior Jesus Christ.

PRAYER:

Father God, I know there have been trying times with the enemy doing his best to attack and destroy Your people. I thank You for deliverance out of the enemy's hand. I thank You for bringing things that occur in the dark to the light; thank You for confirmation and revelation. Lord, I ask that You bring forth restoration of peace, love, kindness, togetherness, joy, and happiness amongst Your people. I thank You for prevailing in ALL of my situations. Lord, bind the spirit of division, confusion, jealousy and insecurities. Heal families and relationships. Father, I ask that You work out our situations according to Your Will. To God be the Glory! Lord, I thank You for fighting battles won and those to come. Lord, I ask that You decrease me and increase You in my daily walk with You. I love You, Father, and I trust that what I pray and ask for will be done according to Your perfect will for me in my life. I thank You for peace in the midst of the storm. Lord, give me what to say and do, that I may honor You at all times. Lord, I thank and appreciate You for loving me in spite of ALL of my faults. I repent and ask for forgiveness of any and all sin I committed knowingly and unbeknownst to me. I thank You for continuing to speak a Word into my heart and soul that I am able to share with others. Lord, I pray for those who are not aware that the enemy is using them by working through them to destroy ALL that which You birthed, created, and built. I know Your Word does not turn void and that what You began will also be what You complete. With a heart of thanksgiving, I will bless thee, Oh Lord. In the name of the Father, the Son and the Holy Spirit, I pray. Amen.

✝ ✡ ☪ ☯

VERSE:

And we know that all things work together for good to them that love God, to them who are called according to his purpose.

—Romans 8:28

THOUGHT:

Family, rejoice!!!!!!!!!!!! No matter what is going on, you can rejoice in God's care, love, peace, wisdom, power, mercy, grace, and faithfulness. There is a purpose behind every problem that you encounter. Because we don't serve a distant or detached God, He is always there with us through each problem that we encounter. Do you realize that you are transformed by trouble? If you try to escape or avoid problems in your life, you delay growth and your deliverance. You go into a state of denial and avoid dealing with the problem altogether. It's for your own good when you go through rough patches. Any time the enemy means something for your bad, God intends it for your good. It all works out when you love, seek, trust, lean, and depend on God, regardless of what your circumstances look like. The trial is for God's purpose, NOT yours, according to how, when, and why God called you.

We exist for God's purpose for us, not our purpose for Him! Focus on God's plan/purpose for your life, not the illnesses, financial difficulties, problem children, your pain, your job, your relationships/marriages, or the plans you make for yourself. Look to the hill from which cometh your help, as your help comes from God and God alone. If you look to the world for help, where has it led you? If you look to yourself for help, where has this led you? But when you look to God, your expected end is much different. You will find rest, joy, peace, happiness, love, understanding, growth, prosperity, fruitful multiplication, and most importantly, you find LIFE! Therefore, endure, look ahead, have faith, trust God, rejoice, refuse to give up, and GROW UP knowing that your problems won't last always. Your reward, on the other hand, is eternal and gives God the glory, which lasts FOREVER. If any of you have had the type of life that I have had, I am praising and thanking God right now for it. I suggest that you do the same.

PRAYER:

Lord, I come to You this morning according to Your purpose and will for me in my life. I thank You for the pain Jesus suffered on the cross, as it is a reminder to me that His suffering is far greater than anything I will ever encounter. Lord, I thank You for endurance, patience and persistence, for without each of these characteristics, I will not be able to see my reward that You have for me in heaven. Lord, thy will, not my will, be done in my life. Allow me to get the lesson to be learned from my trials, tribulations, sufferings, and problems. Lord, I ask that You bind the "why me" spirit in Your people and develop the "why NOT me" spirit. I understand that the "why Not me" spirit leads me to Your purpose for my life. I thank You for choosing me for this journey with all of its valleys and mountaintop moments. I thank You for trusting my faith enough to try me. Lord, I thank You for I know that I suffer and go through for YOUR glory, as this is YOUR will for me in Christ Jesus. Lord, I thank You for EVERY problem in my life that has caused the greatest growth in me that has led me to a great growth in You. Lord, I pray that every eye that reads this prayer experiences You in a mighty way in their lives and that they live their lives, which includes suffering, according to Your purpose for them in their lives. Lord, I ask that You continue to set free and deliver us in the name of Jesus. Amen and Amen.

✝ ✡ ☾ ☯

Follow peace with all men, and holiness, without which no man shall see the Lord.

—HEBREWS 12:14

And the very God of peace sanctify you wholly; and I pray God your whole spirit and soul and body be preserved blameless unto the coming of our Lord Jesus Christ.

—1 THESSALONIANS 5:23

THOUGHT:

God instructs us to follow peace, which means peace won't find you; you have got to pursue peace. The more you find yourself in confusion or strife with people all of the time, you need to take a look at yourself and find a way to bring peace in your life. You must also pursue holiness. The reasoning behind this is that you will not obtain peace or wholeness until you embrace holiness. When you become whole, you no longer sin and you will have peace within your life. Realize this occurs as a direct result of your walk with God. When you begin to present yourself holy unto God, then you will become whole within yourself. Out of wholeness comes holiness and with this comes power. I have found that many people often get married or hook up with each other, in their minds, to become whole. They don't realize you can NOT become whole or one with another person until you are already whole within yourself.

Until this occurs, people really need to stay single, work out their issues, enjoy themselves, enjoy their lives, get saved from sin and get saved from people. Don't look for your better half; look for your whole other. You must be whole and the other person must be whole in order for you to become "ONE." Wholeness should be an assignment of every single person and every married person who now know; they didn't marry their better/other half. Having peace in God makes you whole and complete in God. You must live in the presence of God, allowing God to abide in you via His Word, as well as you operating in the obedience of God's Word until you are made whole. Nothing is to be missing or broken. To become holy in God you bring yourself in line with God. You become one with God in mind, body, soul, and spirit. If you don't line yourself up with God and you line yourself up with people, you will live a miserable life. Therefore, don't line yourself up or live your life for people because God is good for sifting and shifting people out of your life. Can you imagine how it feels/will be when you have based your life on a person and God takes that person from you, how your life will be then? If you looked at this person as half of you, then you will live a half existing life.

Family, I desire that we live peaceful, holy, WHOLE lives in God with the presence of people in that life. I love you all; have a blessed life. I am sure to have a blessed one as well. Pray for me and I will continue to pray for each and every one of you. Peace, Nise

PRAYER:

Lord, I pray for peace in the midst of storms brewing and lingering in the lives of Your people. Father, bind the devil/enemy on every hand. Lord, please get rid of confusion and strife amongst Your people. Lord, I pray for the restoration of peace, love and happiness. Thank You, Lord for Your working people; bless their environments that they are able to be representatives of You in chaos. Lord, I thank You for my family; keep them in the bosom of Your comfort and protection. Father, I thank You for wholeness, peace, and holiness. Thank You for speaking a word to my heart, soul, and spirit. Father God, You know what each of us on this prayer list stands in need of today. I ask that You stand in the gap for all of us and give us the desires of our hearts according to Your Will for us in our lives in the name of Jesus Your Son. Amen.

✝ ✡ ☪ ☯

*THAT which was from the beginning, which we have heard, which
we have seen with our eyes, which we have looked upon, and our hands
have handled, of the Word of life; (For the life was manifested, and
we have seen it, and bear witness, and shew unto you that eternal
life, which is the Father, and was manifested unto us;)*

—1 JOHN 1:1-2

So then faith cometh by hearing, and hearing by the word of God.

—ROMANS 10:17

THOUGHT:

Do we really know and understand the blessing we are living
under? The fact that God's Word will accomplish what it is sent
out to do; God won't stop in the middle of a job/an assignment.
He will not give up on you. He will keep at us, keep taking us
through storms, trials and tribulations, valleys and mountaintops
until we are balanced in our thoughts and whole in our judgments.
The beauty of this is that when God is done with you or even
takes you from glory to glory, NO one will believe that you are
you. No one will believe that you came from the pits of hell as
you now have the glory of heaven on your face. God covers us
with the Blood of Jesus even when His Word is working on us,
which means we haven't arrived yet. The privilege is you are blessed

with the opportunity to change or remain the same. Praise God for His unfailing love. When God sends and speaks His Word to you, He is able to change your thoughts and behaviors. Our thoughts can only be healed by the Word of God. He takes our thoughts and reconstructs them to be like His. This is where our faith comes into play. Faith comes by hearing the Word of God. You must have faith in order to believe and receive that whatever God says, He WILL bring it to pass. God's Word gives us the power and grace to obtain the opportunity to escape and go on with our lives.

PRAYER:

Lord, I thank You for sending Your Word. I thank You that I am not only a hearer of Your Word, but I am also a doer of Your Word. Father, I pray that You continue to give me what to say and do according to Your will. Lord, I thank You for You are not done with me yet and that You won't stop making me until I am complete in You. Thank You for the healing of illnesses in the name of Jesus. Father, I ask that You strengthen my body in the midst of other ailments, that I am covered and won't be affected in the name of Jesus. I praise Your Holy Name. I count ALL that You have promised me to come to pass in this lifetime. I pray and ask You to save, set free and deliver Your people from their minds. Allow them to experience walking with You by faith as You transform their minds and behaviors. Lord, I desire to present myself as a living sacrifice, holy unto You, Lord. Bind the devil as this word is trying to be blocked to be sent out to the masses. Lord, may You place it on someone's heart to distribute what is written of Your Word daily in the precious name of Jesus, I ask these and all blessings. WE will NOT be defeated. Amen.

✝ ✡ ☪ ☯

For God so loved the world, that he gave his only begotten Son, that whosoever believeth in him should not perish, but have everlasting life.

—JOHN 3:16

He that spareth his rod hateth his son: but he that loveth him chasteneth him betimes.

—PROVERBS 13:24

THOUGHT:

When people celebrate love with the slated holiday of Valentine's Day, I would be remiss if I didn't address the fact that I celebrate love every day of my life. I pray that you all do the same. In all of the celebration and sharing of love that we experience, there is NO greater love than the love we receive from God. This brings to mind one of my favorite songs. "Jesus went to Calvary to save a wretch like you and me, that's love. That's love. They hung him high and stretched him wide, he hung his head and then he died. That's love. That's love. But that's not how, the story ends, cause three days later he rose again. That's love. That's love." How many of us are willing to lay our lives on the line so that another may live? Are you willing to die for Christ as He died for you? I know for some this may be a disturbing question. Know that God doesn't expect us to physically die for Him. We are expected to die from sin and our old wicked ways in order to live in God eternally.

Some people are addicted and obsessive with the person they are currently linked to in their loving relationship. If you are dependent on anything or anyone other than God to create a sense of wholeness in your life, then you are abusing the relationship you are in. Your love for that person is out of need for you to feel whatever gratification that you get. You are a taker and not a giver. Love is giving, as to why God GAVE us His only begotten Son. God proved His love for us, not out of His need of us or our love, but out of His giving to us because He loved us. We should operate in this same premise. We should love just because we desire to give love, not because we need anything in return for the love that we give. Now most of us want to just embrace the lovey-dovey side of love. We don't want to deal with the uncomfortable side of love, that challenges and chastises the negative behaviors and attitudes that come along with those whom we love. You must understand that when you allow your child/children, mate, husband, wife, siblings, family or friends to do whatever they want out of fear they won't love you or they will think that you are mean, or they will think you are not the "cool" parent or for whatever reason(s), it has moved us as a people away from checking our children's/each other's unruly behaviors; the environment that we are truly creating is not one of love but that of HATE.

I didn't use the word of my own accord, as you see above it's in the Word as noted in the above scripture of Proverbs. Spanking, chastising, yelling and punishing has, I am sure, always been a hardship for parents or others to engage in. Hence, the notably stated words during a whupping, "This is going to hurt me, more than it's gonna hurt you!" It's not what they wanted to do but what they needed to do to regain order over your actions and life. I thank you, Mommie (Lady Bug), for any and every WHOPPING, chastisement, yelling and punishment that you gave to me. Love is giving and you gave me what love is. Thank you for loving me enough to correct me and making sure I wasn't less than what God intended me to be. I see it as your gift to me and I appreciate you for it.

Family, I urge us to go deep and way back to how our ancestors LOVED each other. This will take us back to the 1900s, slavery, and biblical times. Embrace the legacy of love that we were to gather, keep and allow to grow that we would not be people of self-ishness but people of selflessness in our Lord God, Jesus. I truly love each of you today and always. Peace, Nise

PRAYER:

Father, I ask that You bless Your people today on this love-filled day. Let them experience and give love like they have never known and shown before. I thank You for the love of my family. Lord, I thank You for loving ALL of us so much that You gave us the best possible gift that we could have ever desired for ourselves and that is eternal life from Your love via Your Son. Lord, let not this day of love be in vain but be a testament of what You desire us to do on a daily basis. Lord, help me to love the seemingly unlovable. Lord, I have hid Your love in my heart that I might not sin against You. Thank You for saving me, thank You for guiding me. Lord, I thank You for sending me the man you ordained me to love in my life. He has shown me unconditional love and I desire to provide him with what he has given to me. This is my personal prayer. Lord, I pray for all of the married couples who show love and understand love as a gift from You. For He who finds a wife finds a good thing. Lord, for those waiting patiently for love, let them know and understand that the love You have for them will ALWAYS supersede the love of man. Father, be the lamp unto our feet and the light unto our path. We love You and praise Your Holy name. I pray in the mighty name of Jesus, Your first love and my first love. Amen.

✝ ✡ ☪ ☯

For the love of money is the root of all evil which while some coveted after, they have erred from the faith, and pierced themselves through with many sorrows.

— 1 TIMOTHY 6:10

Daily God deals with us about love. Love of Him, love for one another, love of our children, love of ourselves and now the love of money. We must realize that prosperity equals wholeness, which encompasses the emotional, physical, spiritual and financial state of your success. That is why people who lack emotional love, physical good health and or are spiritually dead but have a lot of money are not whole and they tend to have problems after problems. You may be prosperous in one area, but there is a need for us to be prosperous in all areas in order to be whole. People are often mistaken about what this scripture is saying. People think that God is saying that we are not to have money because it makes us evil. That is not the case.

It's the LOVE of money that is the problem; that is the root of the evil. People love having money, spending money and the pursuit of money more than they love God or others. They are the people that attain financially successful lives but are very unhappy. They may not show it, but deep down inside and behind closed doors, they are lost and miserable. They are rich with materials but poor in the greatest of all commandments and that is charity, which is love. They tend to occasionally let their money go in droplets to make themselves feel like they are doing something for others. Begin to look at what you want your money to do for you. Money without purpose is materialism. Reveal what your motives are about the money that you have or you wish to attain. Understand God channels money to you in order for you to be a blessing and attain the life He purposed you to have. You really need to write down what it is you want your money to do; this is when you will find out what your motives are about money. Motives are critical for what you do and why you do it. Not knowing your motives can lead you into doing the right thing for the wrong reason. This leads to destruction. You may ask why and this is the reason: you help someone less fortunate than you, maybe pay a bill for them; it is the right thing to do as we are instructed in the Bible to help those who are in need. But what is your motive behind it? Is it done to be seen by man, to be praised by man? You did it to pat your own self on the back. You did it because it is what God says to do and with your whole heart, you desire to DO as God would have you to do. If your brother needs food, feed them. If your brother needs clothing, clothe them. You do it because it is what you should do because you are able or blessed to do it. You don't do it with the thought in the back or front of your mind that now this person owes you something or that you will gain anything from man or God for doing what is right to do.

If God, whom by ALL things are given, were to operate like this, a lot of us would be in major debt. Way more debt than the trickle of debt the blessing(s) you have given to others caused. Don't allow money to rule you, as this occurs when you LOVE money. Again, it's not the possession of the money that is the problem; it's the LOVE of the money that is the problem. If you wonder why God doesn't seem to bless you financially, it may be due to your motives of having money in abundance is impure. Money is designed to be the vehicle to do what God has called you to do. True success is fulfilling the assignment God called you to do. Know what God has assigned you to do; this directly correlates to how much resources He provides you to do it with. To whom much is given, MUCH is required. Family, don't be defined by what you have, but measure your success by WHO's you are and who you are. Don't get me wrong, money gives you options, but make sure the options you take are of God. Spend more time, energy and money on the building of the Kingdom of God than on yourself. When we do, this is when we will attain true God-given success. You can truly have it ALL in Christ. I pray to be so blessed.

PRAYER:

Lord, I pray that I utilize the resources that You provide me with to be a blessing to Your people. Lord, keep me humble in the attainment of financial blessings from You. Guide me to do what You will have me to do with these blessings. Lord, I pray that I have been faithful in my giving in the form of tithes, being a financial blessing to others, and doing what is needed to financially take care of myself. I pray that I make money and I don't allow it to make who I am. My treasure is in You, therefore, according to Your Word that is where my heart is as well. Lord, bless Your people according to Your riches in Glory per Your Will. Lord, remove the spirit of materialism that I see so many of Your people suffering from. My prayer today, Father, is that You reveal to Your children Your desires for them, that they are no longer walking aimlessly not knowing what it is that You will have them to do.

Lord, I thank You for allowing me to be a blessing to others. I thank You for placing those in my life that have been and continue to be a blessing to me. I know there were times I didn't know how I was going to make it and You sent Your people to assist me in every need that needed to be met; whether it was financial, emotional and spiritual. Lord, I thank You for keeping me and being on my side. For if You had not been on my side, I don't know where I would be. I thank You for my being lost so that I know what it is to be found. I pray this prayer for myself and all those who have prayed this with me, that we may be blessed in order to fulfill what it is that You would have us to do for the building of Your Kingdom. In the awesome name of Jesus, I pray. Amen.

✝ ✡ ☪ ☯

Submitting yourselves one to another in the fear of God. Wives, submit yourselves unto your own husbands, as unto the Lord. For the husband is the head of the wife, even as Christ is the head of the church: and he is the saviour of the body.

—EPHESIANS 5:21-23

Therefore as the church is subject unto Christ, so let the wives be to their own husbands in every thing. Husbands, love your wives, even as Christ also loved the church, and gave himself for it;

—EPHESIANS 5:24-25

So ought men to love their wives as their own bodies. He that loveth his wife loveth himself. For no man ever yet hated his own flesh; but nourisheth and cherisheth it, even as the Lord the church.

—EPHESIANS 5:28-29

THOUGHT:

You will note that I separated these verses. I did this because so many times they are spoken in separate context, even though each verse gives instruction in support of the other. Family, men and women are quick to say that women are to be "SUBMISSIVE" to their husbands. They don't elaborate to the contingency plan God instructs before that verse and after that verse. But there is a contingency to this. We are to submit ourselves to each other as people in general in fear/reverence for God. Then in conjunction to this, women are to be submissive to their husbands as they are submissive to God. Though the husband is the head of the wife, God is the head of us all. Therefore, how do we expect this to go down, if the woman isn't first submissive to God? Secondly, it gives the husbands instructions to love their wives as Christ loved the church and gave himself for the church. Are men willing to go the full ten yards for their women as Christ did for the sake of love?

Men are further instructed to love their wives as they love themselves. Scripture suggest that if the man hates his woman he must hate himself. The man is supposed to love, honor, protect, nourish and cherish his woman as God loves, nourishes, protects, honors and cherishes each and every one of us. The submission of the woman unto the man is a direct correlation of how the man who is the head and leader first presents himself to his woman. I am sure I can speak for a majority of women, as I had this conversation with many women, we would NOT have a problem being submissive to a man if he loves us the way in which God intended them to love us. But because most men do not engage in loving their women in the manner in which God intended; submission of women to them is lax. They are the leaders and women will follow their lead. I have never seen the head of anything go in one direction and the body doesn't follow it. So the next time anyone wants to debate the issue of wives being submissive to their husbands, please note the responsibility of the men in this equation. Read the scripture in its entirety to obtain the full thought content of the scripture presented.

PRAYER:

Lord God Almighty, I come to You this morning praying for

love. I ask that You pour Your spirit of love into the hearts, minds, bodies and souls of Your people reading this prayer. Father, as I seek You daily on this subject, place in my spirit what it is that You will have me to do. Lord, I pray we learn the value and become obedient to the spirit of submission, that we might be first submissive to You. Thank You for life, love, the power of prayer and peace. Lord, we seek Your face for Your Will in our lives. Lord, some of us need to hear a Word from You. I ask that You touch the lives of all who have come under the subjection of this prayer in the name of Jesus. Amen.

✝ ✡ ☾ ☯

VERSE:

Happy is the man that findeth wisdom, and the man that getteth understanding.

—PROVERBS 3:13

THOUGHT:

Those who are not married may have been a bit puzzled by the Word and message shared. The single people probably feel that the information does not pertain to them, and the married people feel like they know it already. The real issue isn't about what doesn't pertain to you or what you know; it is, however, that we gain wisdom and understanding by practicing what we should know and what should pertain to us. To my single people, most of whom are in relationships or desire to be in a relationship, you have to realize that if you don't start gaining the knowledge and wisdom of what is needed to know to be a wife or husband from NOW by submitting yourself to God, you will have the hardest time living the scripture Ephesians 5:20-30 as it is written and expected, that we as followers of Christ are to do. You will have a difficult time submitting to authority on your jobs and in your personal lives. You have to begin to learn the process as well as the importance of submitting early on, preferably before you get into a relationship and marriage. God is a God of order. When things are done out of order, it causes confusion and we are all aware that God is not an author of confusion. Confusion is of the enemy. Having this mindset early on will assist you in submission toward others as God instructs us to do.

Now for my married people, most of whom are not practicing submission toward each other, mainly due to the fact the men are not in their roles as the true head of households. It's not just about making sure your family is being taken care of financially, but as the head, you are expected to lead. As the head the rest of the members of your body will only perform what you want them to perform. This only comes by your leadership. If your head goes left, the only way your body is going to go in the opposite direction is if it's detached from your head. Now I really don't think the head can and will accomplish much if this happens. The head must be attached, connected to exhibit good communication and cooperation to the body in order for the body to do what is necessary to accomplish a common desired goal. This means, brothers, you need your members, whether it's your wife, woman, children, parents, loved ones, or even your spirit to make things come into existence for your life. So why is it that men feel they can accomplish all they desire to especially if they are in a relationship without first showing leadership in the area of a loving relationship? If you are truly committed to God in your hearts, you would not have a problem being the first to apologize, show affection, show love, show respect, show leadership, show forgiveness, show faithfulness, show vulnerability, show compassion, show concern, show empathy, show sympathy, show strength, and if I left anything out, just think about whatever it is you feel your woman is lacking. Show that first as the example and watch her fall in line to do what it is that God is expecting her to do and what you desire of her. This will also apply with every other aspect in your life. If you show others the nature of your ways and how you expect to be treated, first by treating others in the manner you desire to be treated, you will see that others will do what God is expecting them to do, as a direct response to your behavior.

And ladies, if we start from the beginning to follow what God has instructed us to do, that when the head is doing as he should, in accordance to God's laws, then we would have a much easier life as well. We would submit like there is no tomorrow. I have discussed love shown in many ways, the love of money, the love of your children, the love of your significant others, the greatest love of ALL, God's love with the gift of Jesus, our love of one another, God's unfailing love, and the love of peace. Family, until WE begin to operate in God's Will through submission by way of obedience, we will not be happy. I desire nothing less than for all of us to have a peaceful, loving happy life! Let's begin and for some of us, continue walking in God's Will for us to attain ALL that God desires for His children. This will occur when we find wisdom and further gain understanding of God's Word as our guide for a happy, prosperous, healthy, peaceful and loving life. Family, as always be blessed. Love you all, Peace, Nise

PRAYER:

Lord, I seek Your face early in the morning praying to find You. I am humbled by Your instructions to me, even those that may or may not apply to me today but I know, will apply to me sometime throughout my life. Thank You, Jesus, for submission. I have found that it isn't the worst trait to exhibit but quite the contrary, it's one of the best to exhibit. Lord, I ask that You continue to guide us in the way You desire us to go. I know that Your people desire to seek Your face daily as so many on this list won't start their day without Your Word or prayer. Father, I thank You for Your grace and mercy throughout this journey we call life. Lord, I love You with my whole heart and with my whole heart I desire to see Your face in mine, I desire to live according to Your statutes and will for my life. Lord, bless Your people as we seek You today and forever more. Let us find peace and for those who have peace, allow us to maintain peace. Lord, I know that in the process of serving You that trials and tribulations WILL come. Father, I ask in advance for the victory over them all. Thank You for a grand VICTORY over the devil. As You said in Your Word, if we resist the devil, he/she will flee. Thank You for revelation and deliverance. I pray this prayer with faith large enough to believe for all praying this prayer today, in the mighty name of Jesus. Amen.

✝ ✡ ☾ ☯

But without faith it is impossible to please Him: for he that cometh to God must believe that He is, and He is a rewarder of them that diligently seek Him.

—HEBREWS 11:6

Boy, does this scripture speak volumes. First, we have to realize that in order to please God, we must have and exercise faith. As scripture states, it is IMPOSSIBLE to please God without faith. Secondly, if we are to come to God praying, asking, hoping, seeking, we MUST believe that He is God, God the Father, God the SON, God the Holy Spirit, Lord of Lords, King of Kings and the Great I AM! With all that said, we must also believe, know and understand that He is a rewarder of those who diligently seek Him. When you believe the Word of God, it is manifested by what you do, what you say and ultimately how you live. If you truly believe something, you will speak it.

Everything you ever want to know is right here in this scripture. If you want more of anything, you must seek to know God and walk upright before Him; have faith that what He says that you can have, you must believe you already have it, even before you receive it. Doing this shows God just how confident you are in Him, the level of faith you have in Him and His promises to you.

It shows God how much you trust Him and because of the faith and trust that you exhibit to Him, He will reward you with your desires according to His will for you in your life. Note that I said "your desires," but it is contingent upon His will for your life. There are things and people we want to have in our lives, but they are not a part of God's will for our lives; they are not what is best for us nor are they a part of our destiny/our final destination. If we don't trust God and have faith that He knows what is best for us, then He grants us the desires of our hearts. The problem with this is it can be the very thing or person that keeps us from our destiny of what God has for us. We can't then blame God because our lives didn't turn out all gravy. He rewarded you with what you wanted and not what He desired and planned for your life.

It is better to be in God's will than your own. He always has a better plan than you do. So family, when you seek God; seek Him for His will for you in your life. Seek Him to do His commandments, seek His face that you may not sin against Him, seek Him to show Him you love Him, seek Him for guidance, seek Him for His will and not your will, seek Him in ALL that you do and seek Him so that He can be found. This is the greatest of all rewards, to be in the perfect will of God and ultimately and eternally be in His presence.

PRAYER:

Father God, I come to You early every morning to tell You that I love You, to tell You thank You, to tell You that I trust You and to tell You that I have faith in the promises and teachings of Your Word. Lord, I come to You in faith knowing that You are my God. Lord, I seek Your face to be in Your presence, to hear a Word from You and to feel You resonate in my spirit. Lord, I thank You that I am able to hear You speak to me. I love the relationship that

I have with You knowing that it is a personal thing and that I can come to You as I am, possibly close to perfection today and possibly a total mess tomorrow. I thank You for loving me any way. Thank You, Lord, for Your love, as Your love provides me with choices. I pray that I make the right ones. Father, I believe with every fiber of my being that You will do ALL that You said You would do, that You will stand by Your Word. Thank You for salvation, deliverance, restoration, confirmation and most of all, revelation. In the name of the Father, the Son and the Holy Spirit, I pray. Amen.

✝ ✡ ☪ ☯

VERSE:

Love not the world, neither the things that are in the world. If any man love the world, the love of the Father is not in him. For all that is in the world, the lust of the flesh, and the lust of the eyes, and the pride of life, is not of the Father, but is of the world. And the world passeth away, and the lust thereof: but he that doeth the will of God abideth forever. Little children, it is the last time: and as ye have heard that antichrist shall come, even now are there many antichrists; whereby we know that it is the last time. They went out from us, but they were not of us; for if they had been of us, they would no doubt have continued with us: but they went out, that they might be made manifest that they were not all of us. But ye have an unction from the Holy One, and ye know all things.

—1 John 2:15-20

THOUGHT:

Here we go; meat for your bones and souls. Let this one marinate; I don't want you to miss this. This needs to be prayed on and recognized as a true call from God to come out from among them. You were separated from the world when you came to God. Note: if you love the things of this world and you lust after what feels good to your body and what looks good to your eyes, and you live your life in pride, this is NOT of God. We must keep faith and do the will of God for our lives. Know that there is more than one devil and they come in many forms; trust that God WILL reveal each and every one to you in due season. I know we have received the email that states God places people in your life for a reason and if people leave out of your lives, let them go, for if they would have stayed with you on the path that you were going, prayerfully following God, because they left, it is obvious that they were not supposed to be a part of your destiny. I just wanted you all to know that email is of the Word of God.

We need to understand that there are enemies among friends. But, I need you to hold on because what God is going to do for you, is going to destroy the plan the devil has for you from this day forward. The devil doesn't want you to be connected to the right people, which are believers. Nor does the devil want you to be connected to people who are of like minds as you. The devil uses things and people you LEAST expect to block you from your destiny. The devil won't rest until he fuels the spirit of division; he doesn't like UNITY, for where there is UNITY there is strength. A house divided falls apart. STOP hanging with people who don't want to do anything with their lives. You must hang around the right people because there are things and people who are attached to you—DID YOU HEAR ME—who are attached, not trying to be attached, but who are already attached to you, and they are SUCKING THE LIFE OUT OF YOU. The devil wants to bring you to a desolate place, he wants to isolate you, and he wants you to fall after he isolates you. Understand, it's not a myth that misery loves company because it truly does. You need to, as of today, disconnect yourself from people who you KNOW are not a part of your destiny. Stop running after people who do NOT want to be bothered with you. Trust me when I tell you, they WILL hold you back! Insecure people love to hook up with anybody.

Therefore, be secure in who God called you to be and in who

God says that you are. Know who you are and learn how to be by yourself, if need be, until you find out who you are. What this prevents is your inner attraction to things and people that you KNOW are no good for you. Know what's right from wrong and gravitate toward what is right and what we know to be of God. Remember, if people leave out of your life, they were not meant to be there anyway. Pray for the spirit of discernment because folk are being revealed as the antichrist, they can't stick around you because you have God inside of you and they are not of God. If you are not down with what the devil is bringing to the table, then why are you hanging around them, businessing with them eating at the table, conversing at the table and entertaining them at the table. Don't be hypocritical with people just to be around them.

When you cast the devil out of your life, the Kingdom of God will come to you. Trust God and the spirit within you to know all you need to know to clean house and rid yourself of the devil forever. Know and get it in your heads that what God releases you from, you need to stay set free. If you go back or allow the devil to dwell among you, you WILL surely die. And it won't be a physical death but an emotional, psychological and spiritual death. Trust, this is the worst death imaginable. To be living without God is not living at all. Get out and LIVE!!!!

PRAYER:

Lord Jesus, I come to You this morning with a strong spirit of discernment. I thank You for revealing the enemy to me. You told me to tell satan to get thee behind me and out of obedience and faith in Your Word. I did just that and miracles happened for me. Mountains that seemed to not want to move, moved. Problems that seemed to come on every hand dissipated. Father, I thank You for removing EVERY hindrance. Satan, I know that you are around lurking for a way to get back into my life, but I bind you in the mighty name of Jesus. I need for you to know that I see you coming and because I serve a Mighty God who is ALWAYS by my side, I fear NO evil. Lord, I pray to be on one accord with those You have entrusted to be in my life and I in their lives. I pray for unity among Your people. Lord, I take every test that You put me through as ordained by You to make me into the child of God that You predestined me to be. Lord, I thank You because my life in You has angered the devil, but I claim VICTORY over every tactic, trick and area the devil is attacking me in. Lord, I thank You for being faithful, I love You more than I can ever express, but I thank You for knowing my heart. Keep us covered in the blood of the Lamb. I pray that everyone that prays this prayer receives the VICTORY over the enemy NOW in the name of Jesus. Amen.

✝ ✡ ☪ ☯

Know ye not, that to whom ye yield yourselves servants to obey, his servants ye are to whom ye obey; whether of sin unto death, or of obedience unto righteousness?

—ROMANS 6:16

THOUGHT:

God's people, please recognize the role you are allowing the devil/enemy to play in your life. The scripture poses a question because it suggest that you may or may not be aware of the fact that depending on who or what you yield yourself to is who/what you will obey, follow and belong to. The bottom line is, if you yield yourself to God and obey His commandments that He has set before you, He is Who you will serve in obedience and in righteousness in living. On the other hand, if you yield your life to sin/evil ways, then you are a servant to sin which is ultimately of the devil! Which then brings you unto death out of obedience to the enemy. It is posed as a question because it is up to you, YES, up to you, because God gives us choices all day to choose righteousness over sin, right over wrong, life over death and to choose Him over the devil. Therefore, it is up to you as to whose servant you will be. I know that is heavy for some, and it may be a piece of cake for others. But it is a battle all day. It is not a fight that we see coming. It is not even a fight that we see happening.

It is a spiritual battle over our flesh to do God's will, our will or the devil's will.

We know that anything that is contrary to God is not of God, so even if you feel that you are not being led by the devil and you are doing things in your own accord, then you are deceiving yourself. It's this very attitude and thought that has you all twisted up in the game of life and the trick of the devil that leads you to believe that you have power over the devil by yourself. You are in a fog, you are truly lost if you believe that you have power over anything or anyone, for that matter, unless you are in the will of God and He gives you that power. You CANNOT and DO NOT, operate on your own accord. Either you are being led by God or you're being led by the devil. Either you live/yield your life unto righteousness in God or you live/yield your life to sin, evil and the devil. Do you know who you belong to today? Do you know who you serve today? Well, I know as for me and my house, I will serve and do serve the Lord with my mind, body, actions, soul and spirit!!!!!!!!.

PRAYER:

Father God, Most Righteous One, I thank You that I know to Whom I belong. I thank You for giving me the opportunity to choose life in You. Thank You for Your mercy and grace as I know this, along with my obedience, faith, trust and belief in You will get me to my final destiny with You. Lord, I pray that Your people understand that the enemy will show himself in many ways to deceive them to have them serve him and not You. Lord, I ask that You open their eyes so that they can and will only see the coming of the all mighty Savior. Father, I pray for obedience, revelation, the gaining of wisdom, the bringing down of strongholds and the fleeing of the devil out of the midst of your people. Lord, I thank

You for the VICTORY over the enemy. I thank You for keeping me and those whom I love and hold dear to my heart. Allow those who are to bring forth life, grant them the comfort and safety of your Spirit, Holy One. Heal the hearts and provide comfort like only You can to those who have lost loved ones to violence, illness and natural causes. Father, I ask these things of You because I KNOW I belong to You and I have the right to ask as well as receive what I ask in the name of Your Holy Son Jesus Christ. Amen.

✝ ✡ ☾ ☯

VERSE:

Finally, my brethren, be strong in the Lord, and in the power of his might. Put on the whole armour of God, that ye may be able to stand against the wiles of the devil. For we wrestle not against flesh and blood, but against principalities, against powers, against the rulers of the darkness of this world, against spiritual wickedness in high places. Wherefore take unto you the whole armour of God, that ye may be able to withstand in the evil day, and having done all, to stand. Stand, therefore, having your lions girt about with truth, having on the breastplate of righteousness; And your feet shod with preparation of the gospel of peace; Above all taking the shield of faith, wherewith ye shall be able to quench all the fiery darts of the wicked. and take the helmet of salvation, and the sword of the spirit, which is the word of God: Praying always with all prayer and supplication in the spirit, and watching thereunto with all perseverance and supplication for all saints.

—EPHESIANS 6:10-18

THOUGHT:

For anyone who believes the devil doesn't exist nor does he have place in your life, you are sadly mistaken. The biggest trick the devil ever pulled was to make people believe he doesn't exist. We think that when a person is of the devil that they are operating on their own accord. Well, that is not the case. As scripture tells it,

we don't fight against flesh and blood but against spiritual wickedness. That means we are not fighting the person but the spirit
within the person who is causing the person to act in the ways of
the devil and in the ways of the world. Recognize there is a war
going on in your life. It is spiritual and you must deal with it,
confront it and fight it. Don't give in to the devil. You must understand that your Father is mighty in battle. You may feel that you
are being fought against constantly; well, believe it or not, that is
the case.

Even when you feel as though things are going great, and everything is hunky dory, know that this is when the devil is even more
busy. Trust, he's on his job 24/7. As believers this is how we need
to be on or jobs for righteousness, 24/7. You have to reveal the
devil for who he really is, and that's defeated. That is, unless he is
who you belong to. If you are walking in the world and don't know
God, the devil has a better hold on you than God does because
you have not sought God to know Him and His ways. When you
are in the world, God and the devil are vying for your heart. The
devil positions himself in places you would not believe he would
be in. He gets into your churches through mean members, your
household through unruly children, a cheating spouse or you within your disobedience to God's instructions to you. God is a God
of precise detail. He tells us exactly what we need to do and how
we need to do it in order to fight the devil. He covers all of our
vital organs while in battle if we put on the whole armor of Him.
We are instructed to have faith which acts as our shield, use the
Word of God as our weapon of choice for battle; we are to wear
a breastplate that protects our hearts, lungs and abdomens. Our
salvation covers our head as a helmet protecting our minds, thoughts
and brains. Our feet, which control our coming and going, are to
be protected by peace that we might walk in it in the spirit of

truth. And after you have done all that you can do to protect yourself against the devil, then you are instructed to wait on God, stand still and listen to hear a word from God. Pray like you've never prayed before and the rest is up to Who you trust, of Whom you belong and of Whom you've given your life to.

You can't resist the devil unless you first submit to God. Submitting to God stops the devil right in his tracks. It's up to you to choose what and who you surrender to, but you don't get to choose the consequences that come along with your choice. Realize that you do have power over your choices. Spiritual warfare is deep. God will test your love for Him and take you away/make others leave you when you don't want them to leave. The devil will try to convince you to compromise and not see the person as often as you used to, but you still will see them anyway. Or the devil will have you reach out to a person just to say a prayer to them or to be friendly to them. But what you fail to realize is, that the devil is working in you to be disobedient to God; this leaves the door open for the devil to enter and exit as he pleases. Therefore, when God says something, you are to do it and stand on His Word in faith and trust Him. When satan wants to destroy you, he will put people and things in your life that are contrary to what/who God has for you. When God wants to protect you, He will remove people from your life. When God finishes, you'll know that subtraction is the first step to multiplication. God will remove/take away in order to give you better and more. Satan, on the other hand, will blind you to your destiny and your focus, and he will continue to subtract from your life until you having absolutely nothing. He will have you alone and miserable, possibly even rich with materialistic things, but you will not have peace or happiness.

Family, please take heed and know that your blessing will be held up by God due to someone the devil has sent to destroy you.

The devil will magnify your weakness and distract you from completing and accomplishing what God ordained you to do. Get rid of people who are holding up your success. I know I did!! Remember to dress for the war in the appropriate attire and arm yourself with the appropriate weapon. In other words, don't show up to a gun fight with a knife!!!!!! Family, have a blessed life in God. Stay blessed and pray the devil out of your life. Demand that he flee from your life and if you are blessed enough to have the devil removed from your life, PLEASE DO NOT invite him back in under ANY circumstances.

PRAYER:

Lord, I thank You that I give NO place to the devil to dwell in my spirit. Lord, thank You for showing me how to protect myself when I am going through a battle. Lord, search my heart that I make and choose the right choice. Thank You for revealing the enemy to me. Lord, Your Will and not mine will be done. Thank You for fighting my battles. Lord, bind the devil in our homes, on our jobs, in our families and in ourselves. Father, I thank You for removing people out of my life that You knew were not for me. Lord, help me to keep focused on the task at hand so that I can move forward in my destiny with You. Lord, encourage Your people to pray and realize that a spiritual war is going on to obtain their souls. Lord, don't allow me to business with the devil, cover and protect me from all of his tactics, from all harm and danger. Lord, thank You for winning all of the battles that occurred in my life in the name of Jesus. Amen.

✝ ✡ ☪ ☯

I have set the Lord always before me: because he is at my right hand, I shall not be moved. Thou wilt shew me the path of life: in thy presence is fullness of joy; at thy right hand there are pleasures for evermore.

—PSALM 16:8 AND 11

THOUGHT:

I know there are times in your life where you are going through one trial, tribulation, storm or crisis after another. And at those times you may be looking for God or wondering where God is. I am here to give you some encouragement to let you know that God is with you, but in order for you to feel Him in your presence, you must seek Him. In seeking Him, you will gain a level of comfort from knowing that though you may or may not feel Him, He is always with you. You are going to have to make up in your mind that once you get in the presence of God by seeking Him, you will obtain a closer relationship with God as well as recognizing that God is able. He is able to help you weather any storm, trial, pain, crisis or tribulation in your life. Worship God in spirit and in truth. Seek His face and presence because that is a better place to be in, than one who doesn't recognize or seek God at all. In His presence is the fullness thereof.

Though it is at the right hand that God is found, it is on the left hand that He works and we are. The right hand is powerful and where Christ sits. We have flaws, become weak and are works in progress, so the left hand is where we are going to find God. I know you've been looking for God on your right hand and I can understand why, but the Word also states that when you look on the right hand and don't see God as you perceive Him to be hiding, that it's on the left hand where God does His work. Know that God is NEVER far from the seeker who is on a hunt to be in God's presence. The enemy is who comes along to convince you that God is nowhere to be found. Stand on the Word of God and know that when you seek Him early in hopes that He will be found, is when you will find Him. Rejoice and worship the Lord our God, allow Him to show you the path/blueprint for your life, and there you WILL find the fullness of joy and pleasures in Him. Stand still and firm in your faith, DO NOT BE MOVED; you will receive your reward, your peace, your freedom and your deliverance! Family, be blessed, be good, but most importantly, be good to yourselves. For any of you who are going through anything at this very moment, don't let it distract you from seeking God or believing that you are alone; trust that our Lord our God is with you always. Peace, I love you all, Nise

PRAYER:

Father God, our Host of Host, I come to You this morning seeking Your presence in my life so that I will know what it is that You will have me to do. Lord, I seek Your Will, not my will. Lord, don't allow my feet to stumble. I thank You for keeping me from falling. I love You, Lord, and I lift my voice to worship You with all of my heart and soul. Father, I pray that You take joy in my walk with You. I pray that in my weakness, it's on my left hand that I can find You to gain strength, for Your strength is made perfect in my weakness. Thank You, Lord, for my family. Bless them in their comings and goings, in all that they do according to Your will; bless them on their jobs and their households. Thank You for all whom You have placed in my heart to love; I pray that I never take any of them for granted. I pray for peace, love, joy, health and unity along with this prayer in the name of Jesus. Amen.

✝ ✡ ☪ ☯

VERSE:

Submit yourselves therefore to God. Resist the devil, and he will flee from you.

—JAMES 4:7

Sanctify them through thy truth: thy word is truth.

—JOHN 17:17

THOUGHT:

A great song comes to mind by Marvin Gaye, "...mercy, mercy me. Ah, things ain't what they used to be. No, no." In light of recent family issues dealing with one of our female youth, I would be remiss if I did not give or provide scripture to back up the words of wisdom expressed by four of my cousins, Celeste, Carl, Calvin and Dana, as well as my brother Wayne. The fact is, according to the Word: WE ARE OUR BROTHER'S KEEPERS. This fact also brings me back to the submission of oneself to God, resisting the devil and sanctifying ourselves through truth and the Word of God. Family, I can't stress enough that our walk with God is personal and it must include our children/younger family members. It is our duty as the elders to train up a child in the way they should go (Proverbs 22:6); that way if they depart from the teachings we have instilled in them (yes, this is where planting seeds come into play) when they become older/adults, they will return to the earlier teachings before they went astray.

There are many of us who were brought up in the church and we lost our way. However, because the seed/foundation in God was laid, at God's appointed time, and I say at God's appointed time because I don't want any of us to get it twisted into thinking that we had anything to do with returning to the Father, but at that time we came/will come home to Him, mentally, physically and spiritually because of HIM!!!! Our parents, grandparents, aunts, uncles, cousins, Spiritual leaders (pastors, priests, bishops, etc.) took on the responsibility to introduce God into our lives. And as God gives us choices, as we get older, we begin to make our own choices, where we accept God in our lives and choose to live in Him or we choose to live in the world and in so many ways, choose death. No matter what we choose to do in living our lives, God is forever present even when we don't want Him to be. God is there waiting patiently as our Father, our Lord, our God and our King.

When I look back over my life, and I see the numerous amount of times that I know, if it had not been for the Lord my God on my side, I would have surely been dead. I know it was His grace and mercy that has seen me through every aspect of my life, even when I wasn't seeking His face. My point is more and more of our children are lost and falling into the devil's hands even though strong family values are being instilled in them. It is up to us to continue to teach, minister, pray, lead by example, guide, live righteously before them, offer support and understanding, chastise as it warrants and provide them with as much LOVE and FORGIVE-NESS as our Father in Heaven provides, gives, shows and bestows us. Teach them that the ways of the world are not for them and they, nor do we, have to subscribe to it nor do we receive it. It is the devil's job to offer them/us destruction, but it then becomes their/our job to resist. If we do our job well, all will go well. We must convey to our youth as well as to ourselves to NOT allow the enemy to plug into you and violate you through subtle seductions. Yes, social media pages and some Christian websites are just that. They begin as a positive tool to lure the souls of many and then like the thief of the night that the enemy is, he pounces and ALL are hooked and the website is no longer of God. It is up to you to discern the influences of the devil if you are going to fight and rebuke him. He is using ordinary tools such as your computer, books, magazines, TV and movies to lure you into a lifestyle that is not in agreement with God's Word. This is how the devil plugs into your earthly realm through your life on social media to lure you into lust and remain in the flesh full of lies which causes you not to live your life in spirit and in truth. The devil wants you to believe that you cannot change. He loves prison, bondage and chains. Well, my dear family, I am here to tell you and him that he/the devil IS A LIAR ALL DAY!!! He is trying to produce his distinctive fruit in your hearts, your homes and even in your relationships. Most people lie about who/what they are on these sites. They will say or post anything to get to you. And because you won't think enough of yourself, not to get got, he gets you!

Be careful of what you put into the atmosphere to receive. Make sure that it is of God and resist what the devil is offering. We must exercise the morals and values our forefathers taught, fought and died to give us. Understand that morality is important to God; the Glory of God is manifested only when there is a balance between grace and truth. God doesn't have to punish us in order to heal us; Jesus paid that price. What we MUST do at ALL costs is believe the Word of God and be free. Tell your children the truth. Stop being wimpy parents/elders and leaders. Fathers, tell your daughters the truth about boys/men on how you think and act, SO that they may not be devoured by every male who they come into contact with. Men, also teach your sons to be the men God created them to be. As for us women, we need to know that we are QUEENS. Since when do you know a Queen to walk around being defined by men? She is who/what she is, and that's a Queen. She is not walking around half naked showing her ass (excuse my French) with her boobs hanging out, adorning herself in any and everything that no longer makes her herself. Some women are so far gone from who they are that if they were to remove an eyelash, they/you wouldn't know who they are. Women are hiding behind revealing tight clothing; look at the irony of this statement: they reveal themselves in order to hide their low self-esteem. They hide behind makeup, fake hair, fake nails, fake boobs, fake bottoms, fake lips, fake teeth and the list goes on and on.

Since when was what God created NOT good enough!!! We can't wonder why our younger counterparts are lost. At what point do we instill in our children that they ARE GOOD ENOUGH with how God made them? God created me and I am so pleased. Every blemish, my slanted eyes, my little lips, my big nose, my naturally big boobs (now uneven boobs), my wide hips, flat tail, my chicken legs, my high level of intelligence, my anointing and my cancer-surviving self. I am phenomenal, a phenomenal woman, that's me! Thank You, Jesus. Let's all step into who/what God ordained you to be—Kings, Queens and joint heirs with Christ on the Right Hand of God. I know this message is long and I make no apologies. Family, for those of you who have young children, nieces, nephews, cousins and godchildren who currently use computers and have, Twitter, Instagram, Facebook accounts as well as on some Christian sites, monitor closely the content of pictures as well as dialogue that they send out as well as receive. Our children are not unintelligent, so you won't be able to stop them from going on the sites because they'll just use someone else's account and a pseudo name to log on and communicate with whomever. I urge us to intelligently, lovingly and responsibly offer them wisdom and guidance as to what is or isn't appropriate. Trust, it is NEVER appropriate for a fifteen-year-old girl to be half naked or posing in a sexually suggestive manner, posting sexually charged statements on these sites as to what they would do to the opposite sex. It goes both ways as I have seen sites where the girl is fully clothed and a guy's response has been sexually driven or inappropriate, to say the least. Their mentality is all jacked up. Family, take this information with love as it was given with the greatest love, the love of God because this was not my initial scriptures to share. But the Lord led me to further elaborate on the subject and allowing me to back up my opinion with the Word of God. For through our truth and the truth of God, we WILL sanctify ourselves as well as our children.

PRAYER:

Lord, I give You all of the honor and the glory to You. Father, I come to You in intercession for Your lost, brokenhearted and misguided souls. Father, lead and guide us to the ways of Your statutes. We are losing hold of our youth and I do understand that it is the sign of Your coming. I also rest in the belief that You will not come until ALL that You have promised comes to pass. Lord, I believe in Your people and I know that we can make it into Your Kingdom. Increase self-esteem. Thank You for letting me know that I am my brother's keeper. Let Your people know that they are more than enough and thank You for never letting me ever think or believe that I wasn't good enough. Thank You for my family near and far, providing us with the comfort and peace required to get us through this life. We know that in death for those who believe, there is everlasting life in You. We are all in this thing called life together, sharing You as our Father. We love You and thank You, Lord, for giving us life past one day. I pray these blessings and this prayer in the mighty name of Jesus my redeemer. Amen.

✝ ✡ ☾ ☯

VERSE:

But as for you, ye thought evil against me; but God meant it unto good, to bring to pass.

—GENESIS 50:20

And shall say unto them, Hear, O Israel, ye approach this day unto battle against your enemies: let not your hearts faint, fear not and do not tremble, neither be ye terrified because of them; For the Lord your God is He that goeth with you, to fight for you against your enemies, to save you.

—DEUTERONOMY 20:3-4

Have not I command thee? Be strong and of a good courage; be not afraid neither be thou dismayed: for the Lord thy God is with thee withersoever thou goest.

—JOSHUA 1:9

And Joshua said unto them, Fear not, nor be dismayed, be strong and of good courage: for thus shall the Lord do to all your enemies against whom ye fight.

—JOSHUA 10:25

Thus saith the Lord unto you, be not afraid nor dismayed by reason of this great multitude; for the battle is not yours, but God's. Ye shall not need to fight in this battle: set yourselves, stand ye still, and see the salvation of the Lord with you, O Judah and Jerusalem: fear not, nor be dismayed, to morrow go out against them: for the Lord will be with you.

—2 CHRONICLES 20:15B AND 17

THOUGHT:

OK, people, enough is enough. Somebody is not getting the message/hint/hit on the head!!!!!!! I feel you, but you have got to stop continuing to fight battles that you have NO business fighting. TAKE YOUR HANDS OFF OF IT!!! Leave it with God and trust that He will perform what He is able to perform. Do you ever wonder why scriptures tend to repeat themselves from book to book? Often they say the same thing with the exact words or the same context with the use of different words. I figure it's because God knew we would be hardheaded in these areas. Just in case we miss it the first time, it was written and in order for us to get it through our THICK SKULLS, He repeats His message in various ways. Hopeful that one of the scriptures will grab us and the light bulb goes off and we get it. How many times, how many ways must He say something in order for us to get it! I have given you enough meat to feed off of in order for you to understand that though you want to put your hands ALL over the situation(s) you are currently facing, get off of your high horse and KNOW GOD DOESN'T NEED YOUR HELP!! He is able to do what He said and He has told us time and time again that the battle isn't ours; it's His, that He is mighty and strong in battle, that no weapon formed against you shall prosper, that we are more than conquerors through Him that loves us, that ALL things work together for the good of them that love the Lord, that if God is for us, who can be against us.

Vengeance is mine, saith the Lord, and the fact that God will supply ALL of your needs, not some of your needs, but ALL of your needs according to His riches in glory by Christ Jesus. I can go on and on with scripture after scripture to further prove to you that God is God ALL by HIMSELF. He doesn't require a personal assistant to help Him do anything He states in His Word. God is not like man who says one thing one day and the next milli-second says something totally different. He leaves the lying to the devil and us. I understand the society that we live in because I live in it. But I also understand and know the community of God that we live in and that is a family built and developed on love. When you keep your mind stayed on Him, you will gain a level of peace that would and should prevent you from fighting anything or anybody. God has the final authority over all of us. He decides which battles will need to be won or loss. All He instructs us to do is to be of good courage, stand still, fear not, don't faint/quit and be not dismayed. Stop maximizing your problems/battles and minimizing what God CAN and WILL do. If He said He can do it, as He mentions throughout the Bible, then because He is not a man that He should lie, trust that HE CAN AND WILL DO IT!!!!!!

PRAYER:

Lord, thank You for seeing me through every aspect of my life whether good, bad or indifferent. Father, I ask that You touch and deliver each and every soul that is bound and held captive by the enemy. Thank You for Your Word, as it is plain and is our guide to living our lives. Lord, Your presence in my life indicates that I am seeking You as I should. Lord, continue to help, bless and comfort those who are grieving due to lost loved ones. Lord, provide us with Your wisdom and strength to deal with death and dying in the natural and life in the Spirit. Let those of us that have eyes be able to see, those who have ears be able to hear and those with a mouth be able to speak. Allow only the manner of conversation that is pleasing to You to go forth and give You the praise. Thank You for waking me up this morning and starting me on my way. Thank You for the ability of my being able to work the hours that I do in an effective manner. I love You with my whole heart and with it, I will praise Your holy name. In the name of Jesus, I pray. Amen.

✝ ✡ ☪ ☯

Where there is no vision, the people perish: but he that keepeth the law, happy is he.

—Proverbs 30:18

THOUGHT:

I see this scripture as a revelation on part of what the problem is today with our people. It is as literal and truthful as one can get. With NO vision, you die. And according to another scripture, lack of knowledge causes you to die as well. Don't get me wrong; I'd love to just talk about our black people or my family, but it is talking about the human race. People are forgetting who God said we are, what we can have and who we are to be in Him. We are walking around like poor, uneducated, unruly, unkept clones of the living dead/the enemy. When I say poor, I don't mean that in a monetary sense of the word. Most of the people who I know have MONEY, actually, you guys are rich compared to most in other countries, but you are walking around with a poor mentality. You are lacking vision for your lives, therefore, you find yourself at a standstill in a huge world with minimal amounts of visionaries. As adults this is damaging not only to ourselves but to the people who have to come behind/after us—our children.

Growing up, I truly believe each generation had other people that had preceded them who offered us a sense of purpose, which increased the value of our vision for our lives. For our ancestors, it was the rebellious slaves who ran to freedom; it was Harriet Tubman, a woman who had a vision to save a multitude of people into freedom. It was the heroes of our time/your own time who impacted many into a POSITIVE train of thought and action. Think on your history and who at the time of your upbringing did you have as your visionary to help the vision that God had for you to come to fruition. We must look at when we may believe those types of visionaries, who mind you, did not have to be famous, but were lacking in our own youth. This may be the direct cause for the lack of vision our younger counterparts are experiencing. Martin Luther King, Jr. and our many other esteemed visionaries are so far removed from our youth just as slavery is for some of us, we don't remember the sting or effect of it. We don't have people who actually lived through those times speaking in our ears, minds or hearts. I remember the intimate stories of my personal ancestors and there were things that came to my mind even as a young child that I simply was NOT having in my life because of those stories. There was NO way I was going to be a slave to anything or anybody, which includes money, drugs, sex, a man, a job or other people, for that matter. I have learned that I am not to be a slave to the Lord either. I am to be His child, a joint heir with Christ, a princess, then a Queen in my time with Him. I can't walk around with that truth and then present myself to the world in a manner that doesn't represent who GOD said that I am. Therefore, I walk and live as I see myself. Call it conceit, call it what you want, but I call it my inheritance, I call it MY VISION, I call it my LIFE, I call it GOD in me.

Prayerfully, I am walking that life to encourage both young and old to walk in a manner that is first pleasing to God, then pleasing to oneself, and then as you interact with others, your life is pleasing to them as well. No, we are not to be men-pleasers, but no one is going to say they don't appreciate being appreciated or acknowledged for their efforts.

The difference I see is that our youth are looking for these measures in not only positive behaviors, but sadly, for the most part, the negative behaviors they constantly are shown and bombarded with, as well as what they exhibit. Again, look at the images WE are feeding them. I say WE, because who on this list, including myself, has gone out to prevent the negative images that we all are privileged to visualize and hear from being constantly in every medium (TV, print, movies, radio and real life) that we have from being instilled into our youth and our own minds, for that matter? There are so many things that are just acceptable to us today that we would have literally lost our minds over if it were our daily influences when growing up. I cannot imagine how my life would have been if it were not for the family I emerged from. I was raised, I was reared, I was loved, I was TOLD that I was loved, I was shown love and I felt loved, I was encouraged and MADE to do right, I was taught, I was led, I was told the truth, I was chastised, whipped and spanked, I was hugged, I was kissed, I was spoken to, I was yelled at, I was listened to, I was HEARD, I was rich (and you can take that how you wish), I was accepted and I was made to believe that WHATEVER I WANTED, I COULD ACHIEVE IT, I COULD AND WOULD HAVE IT, IF AND ONLY IF, I DID THE WORK FOR IT, I HAD THE VISION FOR IT AND I HAD TO RESPECT AND PROTECT WHATEVER IT IS THAT I WANTED IN LIFE IN ORDER TO ATTAIN AND MAINTAIN IT. Family, my questions today are, WHAT IS YOUR VISION? HOW DOES YOUR VISION NOT ONLY AFFECT YOU BUT THE MASSES? ARE YOU LIVING YOUR VISION? WHO ARE YOU LIVING YOUR VISION

FOR? DO YOU TEACH THOSE AROUND YOU, YOUNG and OLD, TO HAVE, ATTAIN, AND MAINTAIN THE VISION FOR THEIR LIVES? Now, depending on how you answer to any or all of these questions, it will give us the core root of the problems we are seeing today in our people/the human race.

I am urging each of us to look deep in ourselves to make sure you are living the life God ordained you to live as well as the life you desire/envisioned to live. I love you all. Let's do our best to turn this generation and the generations to come around. We must go beyond each one teach one. We must strive for each one teach many, in order for this thing to turn around. Grant it, it is a hard task, but if it is NOT a vision for us, then maybe for you, it will be impossible to achieve. But I serve a MIGHTY GOD who tells me that I can do ALL things and in Him, ALL things are POSSIBLE!!!

PRAYER:

Lord, I ask that You help people to see their vision for their lives that they may live prosperously, purposefully, and abundantly. Lord, I ask that You speak into the lives of Your people that they may live and not perish/die. Father, it is not for us to know how things went wrong but to acknowledge that they have and do our part in fixing them. Father God, I know that it is ultimately Your job to see this world as you envisioned and created it to be. And according to Your Word, we are right on schedule. But because You said that You will grant us the desires of our hearts and if each heart desired that we do better and because You are a rewarder of those who diligently seek You, then I can be rest assured a change will come. Lord, I come to You this morning with outstretched hands to give You the praise and glory for my life and the lives of Your people. My prayer today, Father, is that we are pleasing in

Your sight. Lord, remove anything and everything that is not You, out of me. Search my heart that I may live in Your statutes, according to Your Will. Lord, I love You and the people You have placed before me to pray and intercede for. I am honored for I believe I am living the vision You have given me. Lord, I want the more of You, so that I can continue on an even larger vein than You have provided me with thus far. I know that it is a mighty request, but I know that in You, I can do all things. I know You give us the power and strength for all that we will endure to accomplish what it is You have set us out to do. Lord, I ask that You heal your land and heal Your people in the name of Jesus. Lord, I continue to hold up my family in prayer. Give us the strength, comfort and love that we need to go through our day-to-day lives. Let us all come together and stay together as the family unit You desire us to be. I ask all of these things in the mighty name of Jesus. Amen and Amen.

✝ ✡ ☪ ☯

And it shall come to pass afterward, that I will pour out my spirit upon all flesh; and your sons and daughters shall prophesy, your old men shall dream dreams, your young men shall see visions.

—Joel 2:28

Praise God, there will be a day of restoration! In the book of Joel, it describes the all-out chaos of the people and the coming judgment of God upon the people of Jerusalem. It talks of the destruction of the land and its people at the hand of God. Truly, all hell is breaking loose, which, if we are honest, we are finding ourselves in that same situation today. The difference is with the Word, we should know what to do in order for restoration to occur. The restoration of dreams, visions, peace, order, love, kindness, good, prosperity, health, strength, marriages, friendships, power and a total restoration of man to God. We learn in the Word that we must repent (turn away from) of our sins. And not just for two seconds, thinking that will get God's attention. God knows your heart and why you do the things that you do. It may take years of us as a people of living righteously in order to prove to God our sincerity of our repentance. Once we successfully repent, God will restore prosperity in all aspects of our lives as well as restore favor. God's favor pours out His Spirit upon all men. Study the

Word that you are empowered to know your expected end. We live to die, but it's how we will be able to live in death that we should be concerning ourselves with. For life on earth is temporary and life with Christ is eternal and everlasting, which I am living for the latter. How about you?

PRAYER:

Most precious Father, Prince of Peace, I come to You in repentance of my sins. I come humble before thee, oh Lord, to ask that You heal and restore Your land and Your people. I have seen with the eyes You have given me the nature and state of Your people, adults and youth alike, and I know it is not pleasing in Your sight. But Lord, I ask that You come in the midst of Your people and restore us unto You. Restore us into the sons and daughters You predestined us to be. I know, Father God, that You have all power over the enemy, but my power comes from rebuking him and I rebuke the devil in the mighty name of Jesus. I refuse for the enemy to have my family, Your people. Lord, I pray that all will come to know You and Your redemptive work on the cross. I pray that what You lead me to bring forth to Your people is meat and not milk for their souls. That it evokes thought, research with a hunger to know You and Your statutes better and that it feeds them in a way that it evokes and jump-starts change. My faith is in You, Lord, and I pray that Your grace and mercy continues to carry us through our day to day, moment by moments in You. Lord, I ask that You not remove Your hands off of Your people. I pray for a better place for our future generations to come, that they will be wiser, not weaker and followers of Your laws to the end of time. Lord, I in no way am trying to rewrite the faith of Your people, but I boldly come to You asking what You said I can ask, which is anything in the name of Jesus. This is my one true desire—that

WE all make it into the Kingdom, that we all recognize our inheritance and our position in You, Lord. I thank you for life and for those who celebrate life. I ask that You continue to bless and keep all of us. I remain mindful that there are souls that are hurting with the loss of family members. I choose to rejoice as their spirits are now commended to You for I pray that the souls that leave us are believers in You and Your Word. Thank You for wisdom and truth that I may live my life by it. Thank You for loving me. I pray today and always in the name of Jesus Christ, my Lord and Savior. Amen.

✝ ✡ ☪ ☯

Dear hearts, know that whether I send the prayers in writing or not, I pray for you all daily. It grieves my soul when I am unable to touch my family on a daily through the prayers or sending out emails of encouragement, but because you all are embedded in my heart, I can't nor will I ever forget you. I pray you all pray for me, as I pray for you.

✝ ✡ ☪ ☯

Therefore, being justified by faith, we have peace with God through our Lord Jesus Christ: by whom also we have access by faith into this grace wherein we stand, and rejoice in the hope of the glory of God.

—ROMANS 5:1-2

FAITH, FAITH, FAITH. We must have it and exhibit it in our daily walk in order for us to have peace in our lives. I have been blessed in my lifetime to witness peaceful home-going services. There was minimal crying, just a big circle of walking faith. I saw people praying by the masses prior to getting on the road to drive caravanning with one another. I saw children standing hand in hand obediently being quiet and understanding the reverence of prayer and planting of seeds of faith. ALL of these actions are actions of faith. This is what we must become and have in our lives so that when it is time for the Lord to call any one of us home, we have enough faith to know we are going to not only a better place but to the BEST PLACE!!! Where we are going there will be no more hurt, pain, sorrow, sickness or death. We are going to be with the Lord where we will have joy, peace, happiness, eternal love, wellness, health and life everlasting. I don't know about you and I am in no way obsessed with death, but I look forward to the day the Lord calls my name and says, "Well done, thou good and faithful servant; sit down and take rest." I can and will wait for that day as I know God is NOT ready for me yet. But when He is, I live my life to be ready for that in the twinkling of an eye moment, I will be caught up in Him. I understand that we all have particular problems based on where we came from. And ultimately we have got to deal with it. In God there is no problem that can't be fixed. In God, there is cohesiveness. There is no such thing as a black church or a white church, there is only ONE church and it was purchased by the blood of the Lamb. We are all ONE church in Christ Jesus. In the kingdom of God there is no social status. In the Bible there are names of purity and names of pure sin listed next to one another or placed in the same Word. For example, the Word speaks on Rahab and Mary Magdalene, both sinners as much as it speaks upon Mary the Virgin Mother of our Savior. This all comes with the faith they possessed in God. Faith is the only thing in this world that gives us an equal opportunity to come to the Lord.

God doesn't care about your gender, how much money you make, how thin you are, how much weight you've gained, if you're poor by man's standards (because we are all rich in Christ), if you are morally correct or if you are the hardest worker. God looks at your heart. He looks at the faith that lives within your heart that oozes out in your everyday life. Your faith is seen by how you handle your day to day—whether the most pleasant to the most hectic to possibly being the most tragic. How do you stand through the test of time, through life and through death? Faith will release you from the pain you have struggled with, the negative medical reports you were given, even down to the daily frustrations that plague you. If you dare to believe you are the sons and daughters of God, you will find the power to stand up straight and be released of ANY burden that has been placed upon you. When we walk as one in Christ, let me say, you will always feel welcomed and embraced as blood relatives because we are joined by the Blood of Jesus. Know that through your faith and belief that ALL things are possible for God, only if you believe, then whatsoever you think, imagine, desire or dream of, IT IS YOURS. LOVE is yours, PEACE is yours, HAPPINESS is yours, WEALTH is yours, HEALTH is yours, MENTAL STABILITY is yours, LIFE is yours and the ALMIGHTY FATHER in HEAVEN is YOURS!!!!!!!!

PRAYER:

Father of Abraham, I plant the seed the size of the grain of a mustard seed in Your people today for faith. I pray that all that receive this Word are deeply rooted in Your Word. Father, I pray that they recognize that ALL they have to do is have faith and believe. That You are NOT looking for perfect men and women but people of faith. Lord, I ask that You continue to cover us in the blood of the Lamb and bind the devil on every hand as he is still lurking in wait to devour Your people. Lord, You said, that if Your people who are called by Your name shall humble themselves and pray and TURN from their wicked ways, then we will hear from heaven and heal our land. Well, Lord, I come to You humble, humbled by the fact that You have allowed me to see another day before I lay my body down to rest and for others that You woke them up and started them on their way. Lord, WE don't ever want to come before without thanksgiving in our hearts, so we come thanking and praising Your Holy name. You are an awesome wonder, a perfect counselor and a way maker. I love You, Lord, with my mind, body, soul and spirit. I give myself to You without hesitation. Thank You for my entire family. I know that I am blessed because You have blessed me with a family tree that continues to be rooted in You and continues growing in You by the blood of Jesus. Thank

You for letting me see and experience the Word, as You say we are all joint heirs, which means we are all related through Christ and that we are not to look at DNA, as the Word states there are friends that will stick closer than a brother. Thank You for my friends that I no longer call that, but I now call them my family. My extra prayer for today is that Your people can know and experience FAMILY as You have called us to be in You today and forevermore. I ask these blessings in the name of Jesus. Amen.

✝ ✡ ☪ ☯

VERSE:

Even so every good tree bringeth forth good fruit; but a corrupt tree bringeth forth evil fruit. A good tree cannot bring forth evil fruit neither can a corrupt tree bring forth good fruit. Wherefore by their fruits ye shall know them.

—MATTHEW 7:17, 18 AND 20

Now he that ministereth seed to the sower both minister bread for your food, and multiply your seed sown, and increase the fruits of your righteousness; being enriched in every thing to all bountifulness, which causeth through us thanksgiving to God.

—2 CORINTHIANS 9:10-11

THOUGHT:

The Word is directing you to have your thoughts on that which is planted, for it to bring about an expected end of what was planted. A farmer doesn't sow a seed of corn to expect an apple tree. Surely a pear tree won't yield oranges as its fruit nor would an orange tree yield peaches as its fruit. Jesus was letting us know that there are people who would come to you showing themselves to be one way when in fact, they were something else; hence, the scripture, you will know them by their fruit. He is letting us know that you should be representative of who it is that you say that you are. If you believe in God, then you would abide in Him and

His statutes so that when people look at you or experience you in their presence, they will know that you are undoubtedly a child of God. Is your fruit, your life, your walk, your talk, your whole manner of being what you represent to be the manifestation of you being a child of God? If God is the tree and you are shown to be the fruit, are you being shown to be of God? Are you living God's statutes? Are you living the Will of God for your life? Are you a false witness of the Word? Are you living in truth? Are you living a life of a liar? Meaning, are you trying to reap being a child of God, but you're in the world, living the world's ways? Are you saying that you're a child of God, but you're living your life like a heathen? Are you a corrupt tree trying to yield good fruit? As scripture states this is impossible. Can I look at you and see that God dwells inside of you? I don't have to go deep in a field to know an apple tree when I see it. I don't have to guess what it is; I will know exactly what it is when I LOOK at it. I don't have to touch it, smell it or taste it to know what it is. Remember the old saying, "the apple doesn't fall too far from the tree." This should be you representing yourself in a manner that is of your people, your parents, their parents and so forth. This is the same principle Jesus is conveying.

Understand and know that your thoughts are seeds that plant all types of things in your mind that you will eventually act on. Your behavior is the fruit or direct result of what you think. For so as a man thinketh, so is he! You need to water your thoughts and nurture them toward good and not evil in order for them to be sustained. You should want to and be able to eat out of the garden of your own thoughts. So don't plant, grow, feed or culti-vate ANYTHING in your mind that you don't want to eat, so to speak. Know that as a child of God, people, that includes but doesn't limit your children, your spouses, other family members, coworkers, friends, and even strangers on the street, they are all looking at you to be who you say that you are, and you should only be feeding/showing them what you have growing in your field. If you profess Christ as your Lord and Savior, then you should be seen as Christ-like. If you profess to know God, then you will acknowledge His ways and live by them. If Allah, Buddha, Jehovah is who you are representing, then one would expect you to represent yourself in the manner in which you have been called. God's Word and work inside of you is homegrown. SO plant God's good seeds in your fertile minds and according to what grows, it will show God, the world and me how I will know you, what you stand for and who you stand for. We will all know of Whom you belong. This is how the tree is known of its fruit. Let God be your tree and you be His fruit!

PRAYER:

Most merciful and gracious Father, let me plant good seeds that You may know my tree/life by my fruit/walk. Lord, I pray that all praying this prayer today know You in a mighty way. I pray that their lives represent you. Lord, lead and guide us to be who You say we are in You. Dear Lord, I ask that my fruit springs forth righteousness and feed Your people that they may live and not die in sin. I pray that the Word that You have given me in this very powerful and personal way, that it takes a barren mind and allows it to grow in You. That the seed of greatness will explode in every believer's lives that they will harvest this greatness in their children for generations to come. Lord, remove the facade of the wicked and show them to be exactly who they are. I bind them in the name of Jesus. Lord, I thank You just because You're You. I love You with no hidden agendas, You are the absolute love of my mind, body, soul, spirit and life. Thank You for keeping each and every one of us. I ask these blessings and many more in the name of Jesus. Amen.

✝ ✡ ☪ ☯

VERSE:

I AM the true vine, and my Father is the husbandman. Every branch in me that beareth not fruit he taketh away: and every branch that beareth fruit, he purgeth it, that it may bring forth more fruit. I am the vine, ye are the branches: He that abideth in me, and I in him, the same bringeth forth much fruit: for without me ye can do nothing.

—JOHN 15:1-2 AND 5

THOUGHT:

First, family, I pray that you are familiar with the Word/Bible, whether you are or not, this entire chapter 15 is a must-read after your day today. The scripture further elaborates on how we must manifest the type of person we are according to the tree/God that we serve. It is Jesus speaking of the things to come of His life and inevitable death so that His destiny would be fulfilled according to the Word. If you are a part of a system of being and you do not produce the fruit that is expected in order to be a representative of that tree, then God will, in so many words, get rid of you. But if you are a branch of His tree, you will be purged in order for you to be able to continue to produce and manifest good fruit. Do you all understand the process of being purged? This means God will clear and remove things/people out of your life that may inter-fere with the type of fruit you will yield and will continue to yield as a part of the nurturing, growth and development process. This process is painful as it consists of pruning and cutting away of things and people out of your life. And you know it consists of the things and people WE want to hold on to, even when we KNOW they are NO good for us.

The Word has a tendency to repeat itself often, and I firmly believe it's because God, Who is all knowing, knew we would have a hard time receiving the destiny He has put inside of us and quite frankly, we would not get the process the first time around. Some of us are still going through our Exodus experience, in regard to going around the same circle for forty years. Without Jesus dying on the cross fulfilling His destiny of the Father, we would not have an eternity to look forward to. Without Him, we can do NOTHING!!! I came back to this with the hope that all of us needing to exhibit behaviors that are in alignment to what and who God ordained us to be in Him. In order for us to move on and progress as a family, as a community and as a nation, we need to be very clear of what behaviors are being manifested; prayerfully, they are of God. I should know Who and Whose you are when I encounter you!

PRAYER:

Lord, I thank You for allowing me to be a branch to You and Your Word. I pray that my whole manner of being represents You and though I may fall at times, that Lord, you know my heart and make my right in the area(s) I may not be doing so well in. Thanks for purging me, by getting rid of things, ways and people You deem are not for me or my destiny. Father God, with all that You require of me, I pray that I bring forth fruit that is pleasing in Your sight. I pray that I am planting appropriate seeds for the Kingdom of God. Thank You for allowing us to get through another day, let alone a week. Lord, know that I am thankful and grateful for all that You bestow upon me and I gladly count it joy. Thank You for being my husband first, that I may be better able to love and care for the one You have sent me. I pray in the mighty name of Jesus that all reading this are branches of You as well, that we are all joint heirs, sons and daughters awaiting the reward of our inheritance in You. In the name of the Father, the Son and the Holy Spirit, I pray. Amen.

✝ ✡ ☪ ☯

He made a pit, and digged it, and is fallen into the ditch which he made. His mischief shall return upon his own head, and his violent dealing shall come down upon is own plate.

—PSALM 7:15-16

Many are the plans in a man's heart, but it is the Lord's purpose that prevails. The devil sets traps for us that he will eventually fall in himself. For it was not God's Will or purpose for you to be caught up by the enemy. Though you must believe there are some traps God will allow you to be in, in order for His Will to prevail. As with David in the lion's den and Shadrach, Meshach and Abednego who were placed in the fire to die, God allowed these acts of the enemy to occur so that He could get the glory out of the situation, so that they would know that because they trusted God with their whole hearts, He was able to deliver them out of death. Even though evil people plot against you, their plan for your life, your failure, your lack of prosperity nor their plans to destroy your peace, will not transpire, "IF" it is not the Will of God for your life. Now, family, you must also understand that you can be your own worst enemy when you don't seek the Will of God for your life. As you go through your day to day of this life, be assured that IF you are not living according to the Will of God, you may very well be crafting your own pit for yourself. It's OK to have aspirations, hopes and dreams, but those things should align themselves with the Will of God for your life. You will know if you are on the correct path that God wants you to be on when you see favor in your life.

When things seem to go wrong and the enemy tries to distract and discourage you, then all of a sudden, EVERYTHING seems to be going according to your plans or things work themselves out. Well, family, that's God giving you confirmation that what you are doing is of His Will and NO demon in Hell can stop it, not even you. The one thing we must be careful of is to think that WE had anything to do with our good fortune. Even though it may be His Will for us to have the plans we dreamed of, if we don't acknowledge Him as being the process by which we received our blessing, then God can and will stop us dead in our tracks, and our dreams, visions, aspirations or plans, whatever you want to call them WILL not be manifested. Family, though you plan some-thing in your heart and try to make it come to fruition, know that ONLY God's purpose for you in your life WILL PREVAIL!!! Also note that it's not up to YOU to dream for the next person, whether it be your spouse/significant other, your child, your parents, your siblings or your friends. It is up to each individual that you encounter to seek God for themselves for His will for them in their lives. So, stop trying to control and take credit for things YOU, mere mortal; you have no power to control anything. Take YOUR hands off of it! Let GO and let GOD!!!!!!!!!!!!!!!!!!!!!!!!!!!!!!

PRAYER:

Lord, we come to You asking that You make YOUR way plain for us that we may be in Your Will and not our own. Father God, in the name of Jesus, we ask that whatever the enemy cooks up for our bad, that You do as You say in Your Word that You'll make it for our good. We trust and know You to be a forgiving God, therefore, Lord, we ask that You forgive us for any disobedience we have exhibited in not doing as You have asked or led us to do. Forgive us for not saying a kind word to that person when You told us to. Forgive us when we didn't make that phone call to check in on a loved one. Lord, forgive us for our unforgiveness of others as we seek forgiveness from You. We thank You for keeping us from harm and danger as we take this journey in life. Thank You for grace and mercy which brings us through all of the valleys that we take ourselves through. For we know that most of them, we took our own fall, but Father, we thank You for making a way out of those pits and falls. Thank You for making a way out of no way. We love You, Lord, with our minds, bodies and souls. My personal prayer today is that I am truly persuaded that no man WILL come before my Lord and Savior. In the comfort of Jesus Christ, I pray. Amen.

✝ ✡ ☾ ☯

And my God will meet all your needs according to his glorious riches in Christ Jesus.

—PHILIPPIANS 4:19

Paul gives the Philippians this promise only after he has emphasized to them that he had found the Lord's grace sufficient in good times and tough times, in times of abundance and in times of lack. The key to this promise is not just God's provision but also our trust in Him to satisfy what we most need in Christ Jesus. When our hearts yearn to be full of Him, to be pleasing to Him, to be blessed by His presence, to be given the assurance of life beyond death, surely, we can rely on Him supplying everything we truly need! Family, there are some of us who believe that our needs will be met by another person, whether it is a parent, a child, a sibling, a spouse, a friend, or even a job. The truth of the matter is "IF" this is your mentality and the way you live your life, you will constantly find yourself seeking something. You will NEVER feel satisfied, you will NEVER feel fulfilled, you will NEVER feel as if your needs are being met at all because the ONLY person that WILL meet ALL of your needs is GOD! If you find yourself feeling unsatisfied, even though it appears that your needs are being met, look at whether or not you are seeking God and receiving the blessings of life from Him or are you looking to man to fulfill what ONLY God can provide?

PRAYER:

Family, my prayer is that you know from where ALL of your needs are supplied; that from today on, you no longer look to people/others to fulfill your needs, but that you look to our Heavenly Father of Whom ALL of our needs are supplied and met. Lord, I come to You, thanking You for giving me eyes to see all the many wonderful ways You are providing for me and graciously providing the abundance You have poured into my life. I confess that my vision is shortsighted and narrow. I need to see the panoramic view of Your graciousness. Yet the "little" part of Your blessings that I am able to recognize are lavish, gracious and fulfilling. Lord, I know You have blessed me with many more things that I do not see. Thank You for being so generous!! Lord, I ask that You let each and every one of my family reading this prayer today and all of our extended family members, friends, colleagues, passers-by, that You are unequivocally the ONLY source that supplies ALL of our needs. Father God, we thank You for loving us so much that You desire us to lack NOTHING in You. Help us to realize that though it is comforting to have others in our lives, there is only one true ultimate Comforter in Your only begotten Son, Jesus. And when we continually seek Your face, Lord, we will, without a doubt, feel whole, truly satisfied and complete. In Jesus' name! Amen.

✝ ✡ ☪ ☯

VERSE:

And the Lord said, Whereunto then shall I liken the men of this generation? And to what are they like? They are like unto children sitting in the marketplace, and calling one to another, and saying, We have piped unto you, and ye have not danced; we have mourned to you, and ye have not wept. For John the Baptist came neither eating bread nor drinking wine; and ye say, He hath a devil. The Son of man is come eating and drinking; and ye say, Behold a gluttonous man, and winebibber, a friend of publicans and sinners! But wisdom is justified of all her children.

—LUKE 7:31-35

"What shall I say about the people of this time? What can I compare them to? What are they like? The people of this time are like children sitting in the market place. One group of children calls to the other children and says, 'We played flute music for you, but you did not dance; we sang a sad song, but you did not cry.' John the Baptizer came and did not eat {like other people} or drink wine. And you say, 'He has a demon inside him.' The Son of Man came eating {like other people} and drinking wine. And you say, 'Look at him! He eats too much and drinks too much wine! He is a friend of the tax collectors and other bad people!' But wisdom is shown to be right by the things it does."

—LUKE 7:31-35 (ERV)

THOUGHT:

The question here is, is there a way to win their hearts? Jesus was not going to win the hearts of those who had decided not to believe. Jesus and John were very opposite in demeanor and style yet those who refused to believe rejected each of them, oftentimes using their "style" as their excuse to not want to believe. Jesus confronts them and basically says (in my own good ol' cornbread English), "You're not gonna believe because you don't want to believe!" As Jesus so often did, He reminds anyone who will listen that the real proof of character is seen in fruit produced in the life of a person. When you look at the fruit of their lives, both John and Jesus show that they are of God regardless of their differing styles.

The sad part to all of this is that after all of these years and centuries, people are worse today. No matter how much we preach, teach and have available to us, some people will never get it. They will never believe nor will they ever get their lives in order, at least in man's eyes. It's not because they can't; it's simply because they don't want to. They see how their lives are with and without God, with and without instruction, with and without love and they STILL choose to continue in their own way. Not necessarily because they even think or believe their way is better. They just want to do what they want to do in spite of the consequences of their beliefs, actions or thoughts. I am learning to accept what others believe to be truth for them. I don't have to agree nor do I have to get bent all out of shape about it. I am coming to grips with the subject at hand today and that is simply, sometimes there is NO WAY TO WIN PEOPLE'S HEARTS! My point of making the statement is that I no longer desire to be held responsible or accountable for those who choose not to be accountable or responsible for their own lives. People truly are going to do what they ultimately want to do. It is what it is and I pray that we all make it to where we desire to be. Have a blessed stress-free life. I love you all, Peace, Nise

PRAYER:

Father, I come to You with outstretched arms needing a hug/touch from You today. Holy God, please forgive me for judging others based on their personal style and demeanor. I don't want to ever reject, judge, or be unsupportive of Your servants. I desire to have a prayer life that brings forth fruit of You, Father. In addition, dear Father, help my life consistently bear fruit for You. I pray for my entire family; bless us and cover us in the blood of Jesus. I place our lives, health, success and prosperity in Your hands. Your Will not thy will be done. In Jesus' name. Amen.

✝ ✡ ☪ ☯

VERSE:

Delight thyself also in the Lord; and He shall give you the desires of thine heart. Commit thy way unto the Lord; trust also in Him; and He shall bring it to pass.

—Psalm 37:4-5

THOUGHT:

Know that there can be no fulfillment where there is no passion or desire. The desire that causes the passion that causes us to achieve has to be strong enough to make us uncomfortable. The discomfort that comes from the desire must be intense enough to keep the obstacles between you and the very thing(s) that you desire from aborting/abandoning the intensity of your desire. Simply put, you must want it bad enough to survive the process required to attain it. It doesn't matter whether it's a good marriage, ministry, business, a peaceful stress-free life or whatever. The bottom line is there will always be hindrances to overcome. Jesus is our prime example of having had a cross between Him and His goal. The cross wasn't His end; it was His means. He didn't in no way shape, form or fashion enjoy His means, but He endured it!! His passion and desire was for the end. His passion and desire to do God's Will for His life was the driving force that gave Him the power to endure His means to achieve the end.

Family, recognize that the desire that burns and inflames your heart, the desire that is forever in your thoughts, becomes the fuel that will enable you to withstand whatever life sends your way. Your desire and passion when directed and put into perspective will make you a person of great accomplishment. Dare to dream. Dare to desire what's in your heart. Dare to desire what God purposed you on earth to accomplish. And dare to have a burning passion that you are willing to quench and fulfill.

PRAYER:

Father, we thank You for granting us the desires of our hearts. Lord, we pray that we are living passionate-directed lives according to Your Will. We pray that our passion spills over into our walk with You and our quest to have the best personal relationship with You. Lord, allow our desires and passion to be directed toward Your Godly vision for our lives. Lord, please don't allow my passion or desires to die; let them grow so that I can live the dreams You have placed in my heart and the visions that You planted in my mind. Father, I ask that You don't allow any of us praying this prayer to become complacent and give up on Your vision/our dreams because the road to obtain those dreams are difficult. Allow us to tackle all that we do for Your Kingdom building to be done with great passion and for us not to just be doing things by going through the motions. We thank You for all You have blessed us with. We thank You for continuing to protect, guide and keep us. Lord, some people have had trying times and it isn't over yet. Let the pain and suffering that others have endured be a light for another. Especially those of us, mothers and fathers, who have and will go through the unfortunate journey of losing a child. Bless our hearts and Lord, continue to grant us peace and joy as we put our faith, hope and trust in You. In the name of Jesus, we pray. Amen.

✝ ✡ ☾ ☯

Behold, He who keeps Israel shall neither slumber nor sleep.

—PSALM 121:4

Family, this verse is such a great comfort to me. Aren't you glad that God doesn't take the day off? Imagine if you were in a crisis and called out to God, "Lord, help me!" and in response, heard a voice from heaven that said, "I'm sorry, God is not in right now. He has the day off. He is out on the golf course. He took a sick day. He's not here, he's running late, but you can leave a message on His voicemail." Thankfully, God is always at work. God is always available. He is always listening, ready, willing and able to provide us with what we need, when we need it. The other comfort that I have is that God is never late. He's always right on time. God is tuned into your cries, to your hurts and your pains. He doesn't slumber or sleep. You know during Jesus' earthly ministry He was on an agenda. He had goals that He was working toward. He had a purpose He wanted to accomplish. He had people He wanted to meet. He had lives He wanted to change. He had healings He wanted to perform. Jesus had an appointment with those who came searching for answers. And He also had appointments with the forgotten people. We must conduct our lives in the same manner. We must know our goals, live our purpose and accomplish what God has ordained that we were born to do. Know that no matter what is going on in your life, in the world or with others, God is always listening for the cries of His children, just as parents listen for their children. He is our Father which art in Heaven.

PRAYER:

Father God, I come to You early in the morning seeking Your face as I do daily, thanking You for my return of sharing Your Word with Your people. Lord, I thank You for leading and guiding me on this journey called life. I pray that I am living the life You have ordained me to live. I thank You for the many wonderful blessings that You have allowed to enter into my life. Lord, hear my cry when I say we need You today, Lord, now more than ever. Father God, touch, free, deliver and heal Your people in the mighty name of Jesus. Give us strength, courage and wisdom to go through our day-to-day living. Bless those who do Your work according to Your will and purpose for them in their lives. Bless our comings and our goings. We thank You for love this morning. We thank You for life, unity, wholeness, oneness in You and we thank you for family. We pray this prayer in the precious name of Jesus. Amen.

✝ ✡ ☪ ☯

But the Lord said unto Samuel, Look not on his countenance, or on the height of his stature; because I have refused him: for the Lord seeth not as man seeth; for man looketh on the outward appearance, but the Lord looketh on the heart.

— 1 SAMUEL 16:7

THOUGHT:

Let me tell you something that may offend a few of you. So, I will ask God for forgiveness now as I know that is not my goal, but the truth hurts and it will set you free. At least that is what the Bible says. (smile) You can go broke trying to fix what's on the outside not tending to your inner man/self. In turn you will still have the same issues, the same emotional status, the same thought process; you will still be lonely and alone. Nine times out of ten, we take care of our outer beings, to be more pleasing to others because that is what they see. There is plastic surgery for everything known to man except for your spirit, soul, mind, your way of thinking, your feelings, insecurities, attitudes and lifestyles. But who gave us life? God! What does He see? What does God say about you? He sees ALL of you; from your dirty little secrets, to the best part of your hidden heart. He sees your pain, your conflict, your desires, your good doings, your hurts, your worries, your fears, your courage, your strength and your tears. God sees and knows it ALL. He is constantly concerned about you. The question is, are you constantly concerned about you? Not the outer you, but the entire whole you that includes your inner man. The you, you have to face on a daily basis. Maybe I should speak for myself. The me I have to stop when someone gets on that last nerve that isn't so last, but it's the first or only nerve that I have. I want to lose it, but I think to myself, truly, what would Jesus do? I try to live my life in a manner in which I don't offend God. I live my life in LOVE for that very reason.

It is equally as important that my outside matches what my inside is growing into. As I am a continued work in progress and God isn't finished with me yet. Call me conceited, but I know that my inside is quite BEAUTIFUL!!! We need to biblically understand that there are things that bind people. Let's take Sampson with Delilah. It wasn't that he couldn't get away from her beauty. She became a place where he could get rest. He would lie on her and sleep. He was tired and she provided him rest. He needed that desperately; even though he knew she was trying to kill him, he couldn't stay away. The devil will work through people who bind themselves to you and who you bind yourself to that looks good on the outside, but they mean you no good. You can enrich your relationships through your inner beauty. Trust, it's not your outer beauty that makes you attractive. It's something that God puts in your heart that will affect who will be attracted to you and why.

The enemy wants to capitalize on what God put in you. Trust me, the enemy looks for your good so that he can destroy it and YOU!! Family, everybody doesn't mean you good. There are people in your lives, mine included, who have hidden agendas. This is why we must watch what and who we let in our doors. Be as God is with us. He is not interested in what you look like or what you have; His concern is your heart. Be like David, be a mess, know that you are a mess, but continue to seek God for the good that you and He know is in you. Family, stay beautiful, stay watchful, blessed and prayerful. Keep your eyes on the true prize, The Lord Our God. Stop trying to fix what you look like on the outside and fix your inner man to match who God created you to be. Look like from the INSIDE out and NOT the outside in...

PRAYER:

Lord, I thank You for the spirit of discernment. I thank You for the physically beautiful man that You sent me, but I am most grateful for his heart. I thank You for all of the beautiful spirits and hearts I am praying for and with daily. Lead us, Heavenly Father, that we are not bound in any way, shape or form to the enemy and his wicked plans for our death. We know he is not concerned with our lives as he is only here to steal, kill and destroy us. Thank You, Lord, for eternal life in You. We thank you, Father, for Your Son as we are able to be with You when You call for us. Thank You for Your healing powers, family and prosperity. I thank You for each and every eye that reads this prayer today. I humbly come to You as Your child asking that You keep us covered in the powerful blood of the Lamb. In the name of Jesus, I pray. Amen.

✝ ✡ ☾ ☯

VERSE:

And wisdom and knowledge shall be the stability of thy times, and strength of salvation: the fear of the Lord is His treasure.

—Isaiah 33:6

THOUGHT:

It's your time, family!!! You all ought to be celebrating off of this one. Your heart should be filled with a hallelujah praise of joy. Take a look back over your life and think of how God has plowed and fertilized you. You should be thanking Him right now as WE are still here to attest to His sustaining power. A lesser man would not have survived your testimony. The testimony that has given you wisdom, knowledge and strength. Look at the blessings you have right at this moment. Don't take long to thank God for what He is doing, even at this very moment. You are a freshly culti-vated ground full of seeds that were planted inside of you and around you since your birth. Some of those seeds are full of unborn potential. Yes, there is still more of you and more for you to do. He has BEGUN a good work in you, which means He ain't done with you yet! Thank You, Jesus, for not being through with me yet.

Therefore, when you wake up every morning by His grace, cele-brate the fact that you are still here. Understand what a blessing it is to be alive, to be able to feel and be able to taste life. Be glad of that and celebrate what God is about to do in your life for each day. Your heart ought to be dancing on that note. Your blood should be racing through your veins like you're in the Indie 500. Family, we are about to step into the greatest harvest of our lives. Hold on, and take that in. Breathe and savor the moment for when it happens, your life will NOT be the same. The enemy knows you are about to reap all that God has put in you. That is why he has fought us so hard these past few years. The devil is a liar and he can't and won't have any one of us!!! If the devil/enemy can recognize that it is your time, it's time for YOU to recognize that it is your time. This is your wisdom, this is your knowledge and this is your time. All that has held you together, given you strength and stability is about to take off like wildfires. No demon in hell will be able to stop the treasures that The Lord has for each of us. Praise Him. It's OK to SHOUT!!! I know I am. A powerful prophetic move is about to explode in our lives and I feel it as easy as I am breathing this morning.

PRAYER:

Heavenly Father, we praise Your name this morning. We come before You today with hearts of thanksgiving. Thank You for life. Thank You for trials and tribulations, as we have learned, they have molded and ripened us for our due harvest. Lord, we thank You for one another, as no one man is an island. We understand that we are in this thing called life together. Lord, thank You for wisdom, knowledge, and understanding. And for all that we do not understand, we thank You for faith to trust that in You, ALL things are possible and everything is going to be all right. We thank You for the lives lost as they were able to be a part of us and us a part of them. We thank You for allowing us to experience a piece of You in every life that has come across our paths. Thank You, Father, for this ministry. Thank You for Your Word and it being a lamp unto my feet and the light unto my path. Thank You for not giving up on me. Thank You for being a God of not only a second chance but a chance after a chance, after a chance. Lord, I can't thank You enough for all that You are to me. I love You, Lord, with my whole heart. I pray this prayer in the mighty name of Jesus. Amen.

✝ ✡ ☾ ☯

Take therefore no thought for the morrow: for the morrow shall take thought for the things of itself. Sufficient unto the day is evil thereof.
—MATTHEW 6:34

Come unto me, all ye that labour and are heavy laden, and I will give you rest.
—MATTHEW 11:28 (REVISITED AS LED BY THE LORD.)

Family, there are some of you who are so busy living for tomorrow, you're missing the here and now. Don't get me wrong. There is nothing wrong with planning for your future. The problem comes in when you miss living today to worry about it. Savor the life that God has given you. Stop worrying about things that may NEVER happen—good, bad or indifferent. We can plan all that we want, but if it's not in God's will for it to be, it won't be. God operates in divine order, not according to our dreams and aspirations. He honors the desires of our hearts but not necessarily in the manner in which we expect nor the time that we expect it. The bottom line is, some of you are so busy worrying about tomorrow when tomorrow only worries about itself on that day. You all are stressing yourselves out over things you have NO control over. Yes, I do make plans according to how God leads me. I seek the

Holy Spirit for each and every move that I make. As I don't want to do anything on my own accord, I have seen and lived the results of that. You all are working your brains, emotions, fears, concerns, health, and life into overdrive. You are exhausted. Guess what? God knew you would be. Hence, the revisited scripture, Matthew 11:28. Look to the Lord, He will give you rest. He will sustain you. He will take care of you. The key to this is, IF you let Him!!! We ALL wrestle with things. One person's struggles may or may not be another person's struggle. The beauty of this is that God calls those who have a past, those who have struggled with something.

I explained to someone that I thank God for EVERY trial that I have gone through because they have brought me to where I am today. Believe it or not, it's a pretty good place to be. I don't worry about what the Lord is going to have me write to you all. I will close this laptop without a thought of it. I will enjoy what God has done in my life yesterday and will rejoice when He wakes me up later today to start my day. I am not concerned with no day of the week. I will do that when the day comes. Family, our present day brings enough challenges; why not deal with those and concern yourself with all else WHEN the time comes. Regardless of what, you can ALWAYS go to the Lord. Understand that God knows your history/your past and He knows your tomorrow/your future. I just don't envision God sitting on the throne worried about your tomorrow. The question I pose to you is, why do you? God knows you and He is calling each and every one of you. He is calling you out of darkness and into the light. He is calling you to be joint heirs with Christ. He is calling you to follow His statutes. With one being fear NOT, meaning don't WORRY! Rest assured, God knows ALL about you. He is in control. Let go and let God. Put your worries of tomorrow aside and LIVE for today!

PRAYER:

Holy and Righteous Father, Our Savior, help us to not dwell on tomorrow as it is not here yet. Help us to totally depend on You for our future. Lord, forgive us for our unbelief, our lack of faith and our lack of trust in You. For if we truly exhibited these attributes, we would not worry for anything today, tomorrow or in our futures. Thank You, dear Lord, for allowing me to see that my life is worth living today. I'm living and loving this moment because of You. Thank you for calling me on purpose in spite of my past, in spite of my tomorrow, and in spite of what You and only You know my future to be. Deliver Your people, Heavenly Father, of their worries today. Heal their minds. Bless their finances, their bodies, their families, their homes, their jobs, comings and goings and their obedience. Lord, I realize that you have saved us from our pasts and in doing Your Will, we will NOT have to worry. Strengthen us with Your spirit and bind the enemy on every hand. We love you, Lord, and praise Your Holy name. In the name of the Father, the Son, and Holy Spirit, I pray the blood of Jesus over it all. I count it done. Amen.

✝ ✡ ☪ ☯

If you all know the next scripture, you will see that I am sharing powerful seasoning to add to the pot for the prepared meal of God's Word that I have been presenting to you. These seven (7) words should make you scream and shout with such joy and peace. I have experienced some amazing days, and I know the magnitude that this scripture has represented with the power these 7 words represent in my life. I am dancing right now!!!!!!!! Be blessed and have a great life in God. Hold on just a little while longer. The Lord said troubles won't last always. I Love you and I need you to survive. Peace, Nise

VERSE:

For with God nothing shall be impossible.

—LUKE 1:37

THOUGHT:

Oh my God, Family, did ya'll let these seven words marinate in your spirits, in your bodies and in your souls. This is soooo deep. NOTHING, not one thing shall be impossible for God. Who are you putting your faith in? I have to ask, for those who worry, for those who procrastinate, for those who say I can't, and for those who put off the inevitable with the thought it won't go in their favor. I can go on and on about my thoughts for this scripture, but this is about you today. This sentence with those seven words truly speaks for itself. I will leave you with this: This is the main reason I live a VICTORIOUS life. So when you want to ask yourselves why I never wavered in my faith with a diagnosis most lose their footing in, refer to this scripture and you will then understand why my faith and trust in my Father more than doubled. My living with and through all of the side effects of cancer never caused my faith, trust, hope and belief in God to waver. If anything, the Word of God, especially this scripture with these seven powerful words, made my love, trust, hope, belief and faith in God that much stronger.

PRAYER:

Heavenly Father, I come to you daily, praying that Your people who are called by Your name understand, trust, believe and receive that You are the One and Only God of Whom ALL things are possible. Father, let them understand that no matter what their situation or circumstances look like, that if they look to You and not to themselves, that NOTHING that they require or desire in You is impossible. Lord, strengthen those who are weak. Heal those who are sick in their minds and bodies. Touch, deliver and set free those who are bound by the enemy. You have proven to me time and time again that NOTHING is impossible in You. Because I live my life in You, I am finding myself in situations I never even thought I would be in and I am appreciating EVERY experience, good or bad. For I know in my heart of hearts that it is ALL of You, and what the enemy may feel is for my bad, You work it out in my favor for my good. Thank You, Jesus, for my good days far outweigh my bad days and guess what, Family? I WON'T COMPLAIN! Lord, I thank You for this scripture and prayer. I ask that You protect and keep everyone and their households who are praying this prayer. We Love You, Lord, and humbly pray in the mighty name of Jesus. Amen.

✝ ✡ ☪ ☯

I shall not die, but live, and declare the works of the Lord.

—Psalm 118:17

Family, I am not sure where the Lord is leading me, but if these two scriptures are an indication, watch out. Pray very hard because the enemy is really busy in some of our lives. You may not feel the impact of him yet, but he is on somebody's heels. He is about to reveal himself in your life. Get prayed up and fired up. I am finding that we as a people have a flagrant disregard for the welfare of one another. Abuse at the hand of one another regardless to whether it's physical, psychological, mental, emotional and or sexual. It is a disturbing situation to hear of a child, male or female, being abused in any way. It is equally disturbing to me that these children grow up to be adults and are covering a past that is destroying them. They have been dying daily inside and they are among the walking dead. But I challenge any of you that the enemy has attacked in this manner to LIVE and NOT DIE!!!!!!! When we knowingly live in silence of any injustice, down to bullying, we perpetuate, and contribute to the continued victimization of our children, elders, people whom we love that have been victimized. In the medical field we have come to realize that wounds don't heal well that are covered. Stop hiding and covering up that which NEEDS to be healed. It's like having a wound or cut; it needs to be left OPEN to air to heal properly. Whatever it takes, we must declare that God is king of kings and lord of lords. He is stable in His thoughts for us; they are of peace, love, happiness, joy, and LIFE!!!!!!

PRAYER:

Father God, in all that we go through, we thank You for not giving us over to death. Heavenly Father, most gracious One, we praise Your Holy name for the plights of Your people are heavy and enormous. We stand in faith believing that in You, Lord, ALL things are possible. Lord, let the meditations of my heart and the words of my mouth be acceptable in Thy sight, Oh Lord, my strength and my redeemer. Lord, let us not take Your grace or mercy for granted. We exalt You this morning; there is none like You, Lord. Lord, I ask that You continue to deliver and set free the burdens of Your sons and daughters. Lord, help us to realize our past is our past. Move us into the new. Create in us a clean heart and renew the right spirit within us. Thank You, Jesus, for every soul that is living under Your statutes; every soul that obeys Your commandments; every soul that honors marriage; every soul that fears You, dear Heavenly Father. Bless everyone and our family members both near and far. Lord, I will be remiss not to thank You for loving FRIENDS that sticketh closer than a brother. We Love You, Lord, and pray in the name of our Savior, Jesus Christ. Amen.

✝ ✡ ☪ ☯

THOUGHT:

Family, what a relief, we are made strong in weakness. Real success takes place when you are strengthened through trying times. You may feel weak, you may be crying and you may have suffered, but you still made it. We all have flaws and most of us have experienced failure, but it is your faith in God that has you in the place you are in today. If your faith is strong in the Lord, you are living a victorious life. If your faith in God is weak or in question, you are more than likely living a defeated life. I am not talking about having weak moments in your life; I am talking about your entire life. Occasional weakness doesn't affect your overall performance in battle. So in spite of your struggles, your tendency to get off track, and your moments of decreased faith, you can still make it because of your belief in God! Family, lift yourself above your circumstances and struggles. Fight the enemy within and without. Yes, sometimes we have to fight ourselves to stay on track of what it is that God will have us to do. Some of you are your very own worst enemy. Stop blaming the enemy outside of you when it is you that is defeating you. Let's place this in our memory files that when it occurs, we recognize it and get rid of this internal enemy before it grows into a monster you can't destroy. I believe this is what happens when people allow their minds, bodies and difficult circumstances get the best of them, and they live in a world of depression, sin, guilt and shame, and they commit suicide. Be patient in long suffering and remain joyful as the scripture says because troubles don't and won't last always. Your breakthrough is on the way. Keep the faith, trust God with all that you have in you. LIVE, family, LIVE!!!!!!!!!!!!!!

PRAYER:

Father God, in the name of the Almighty Son, we come to You this morning in intercession for those who may be too weak to seek Your Holy face. Father God, with Your all-knowing power, we thank You for providing us strength in weakness. We thank You for allowing us to see another day. We thank You for being in our right minds at this very moment. Thank You for all of the blessings of life You have allowed each of us to experience. Lord, we thank You for protection and the covering power of the blood of Jesus. Lord, this is my personal prayer to You. I am grateful for the family You have placed in my life. I am well aware it is all a blessing to love and be loved and I thank You for the love You allow me to feel from Your people. I thank You for allowing me to live forty years of life with You by my side EVERY step of the way through everything. I thank You, Lord, for favor. I thank You for Your grace and mercy. Thank You for my VICTORIES over the internal and external enemy that tried on many occasions to take my life. Thank You, Lord, for it is obvious You saw fit for me to STILL be here. A fact, Father, I will not take for granted. I humbly come to You professing my love for You and my family. Knowing that without You, Lord, none of this glorious life You are having me to live would be possible. Thank You for my journey, my anointing and my prayer life. Lord, last but not least, thank You for Your Son in whom I now have eternal life with You. It is in Your Son's precious name, Jesus, that I pray. Amen.

✝ ✡ ☾ ☯

VERSE:

Though He slay me, yet will I trust Him: but I will maintain mine own ways before him.

—Job 13:15

THOUGHT:

The Spirit of the Lord is telling me that you all need to get this today. If you are familiar with the Word, you know that Job is going through it. He was a man of wealth with a large family. According to our standards, he had it all. The devil asked God's permission to attack Job because he was a faithful man of God whom the devil felt ONLY trusted and loved God because of his wealth and status. God, knowing full well Job would not waver in his faith, allowed the devil to attack Job but not take his life. Although all of his possessions were taken away, Job trusted God. Though all of his children were taken by death, Job trusted God. Although all of his friends, including his wife, called him a fool for trusting God, Job trusted God. Now I don't know how it feels to be sleeping with the enemy, but Job at this point was sleeping with the enemy in more ways than one. His own wife, whom he is supposed to be one with, did not stand by her husband in his most trying time. She wanted Job to curse God so that God would kill him and take him out of his misery. I don't know about you, but I could not be with a man, spouse, partner or significant other who didn't believe what I believe. But the beauty of this is, Job didn't allow ANY of it to determine his faith and trust in God.

I often reflect on the book of Job, because I too have been afflicted and had things very dear to me taken away. And I found that what the Lord gives, He can quickly take it away, and in the midst of all that I lost, I can STILL trust and believe in the promises that MY FATHER have made to me. I realized I had to be like Job that no matter what was happening or going to happen in my life, I will trust, love, obey, and believe in God. Understand, Family, that God can do anything but FAIL! He can take care of ALL of your needs right now. For the same God that brought you through yesterday can do the same for you today and forevermore. There are things about God you will never understand until you live your life in Him and experience Him. You learn obedience through the things you have suffered. So, don't spend your life stressed out over things you can't handle nor are you supposed to handle; turn it over to God. The way that you do this is you TRUST Him. Family, you've been tied up long enough. You have worried long enough. You have been upset long enough. If you truly want to be free, cut the ropes off of your mind, off of your spirit and off of your situation. I may be a little long-winded, but someone reading this LIFE is depending on this Word written!!!! I feel it in my Spirit and I pray that you all are praying and discerning this with me. For it can be the very person next to you. We must open up our eyes and spirits to see and realize when people are hurting. Not the type of pain they can just brush off but the type of pain that consumes them and takes their life mentally, emotionally, spiritually or physically.

Jesus came that we may have LIFE and have it more abundantly. The devil is a liar and he CANNOT HAVE ANY MEMBER OF MY/OUR FAMILY!!!!!!! I can't express this enough: TRUST God and let it go. No, it isn't easy, it takes work and you need to find the strength to do the work. It is worth it; you are worth it. Most blessings come when you relax and let go. You all know my motto, IT IS WHAT IT IS. If you can't change it, stop worrying about it. If you can change it, then do WHATEVER you have to do to change it. Don't give up, no matter what; you will see a breakthrough if only you believe. All of us believe enough for each other. WE ALL SHALL LIVE AND NOT DIE. I love you, Peace, Nise

PRAYER:

Lord, I know what You are speaking in my spirit is heavy and may be much for some today, but my concern is for the spirit of destruction and death that I am feeling in Your people. Lord, give them enough encouragement to continue to have faith in Your awesome wonder. Lord, keep and bless them. Have your way in their lives that they may be a great testament of Who You are. Father God, I thank You for the spirit of discernment for I know this will set free and deliver someone. I know that Your Word does not return back to You void. I thank You for being an all-knowing God. I thank You for leading me in Your Word. Father God, You know that if this ministry was up to me, I'd be trying to go to sleep right now. Thank You for obedience. I pray that all who will read this know You in the most intimate way as I know You. Family, I pray that you know that your walk with God is personal. It is what you desire it to be. I pray He is your all in all, for He is mine. I thank You, Heavenly Father, for protecting us in our travels, in our sleep and in our day-to-day living. Lord, bless and protect the anointing on our children. I plead the blood of Jesus on every eye that reads this prayer. I love You, Lord, because You are my King of Kings and Lord of Lords. In Jesus' name, I pray. Amen and Amen!!!!!!

✝ ✡ ☪ ☯

VERSE:

And I will make thee a great nation, and I will bless thee, and make thy name great; and thou shalt be a blessing.

—GENESIS 12:2

THOUGHT:

Oh, what assurances God gives us in His Word. God is making a promise to us by saying what He WILL do in our lives. I have never seen in the Bible when God speaks something where He says maybe, might, perhaps, if only, probably or I think. God doesn't use words that will make you believe that whatever it is that He wants you to do, have, say, feel or believe that He doesn't want you to have it, He doesn't want you to be confused about it. He wants you to KNOW. Therefore, He uses words such as He WILL, you WILL, He SHALL, you SHALL. These are words that let you know that whatever it is that God has for you, it will happen. His Word is definitive. There are no ifs, ands or buts about it. I am grateful for His WORD, aren't you? This is our true blessed assurance. Know that what God has for you it is for you! Even though God has made you promises and you haven't seen them yet, doesn't mean He won't perform what He said He would do. It just means it's not His time to perform it for you. It may mean that you're not ready for it, as God is ALWAYS ready to perform what He said He is able to do.

God is ALL knowing, and I personally don't want anything He doesn't deem I should have nor do I want it if He deems I am not ready for it. Furthermore, just because I want something doesn't mean I should have it. There are a lot of people who wanted things and because they didn't wait on God, they have found themselves in a world of trouble. I have no problem waiting on God for what He has for me because of verses like Genesis 12:2. We as a people should not settle for where we are right now for God will change all of it around if you believe. I say if because nine times out of ten, we block our blessings. We step in and mess things up. Stop blaming God because YOU chose not to wait on Him and what He promised for you in your life. He said He WILL bless you, He WILL make your name great, He WILL make our nation great by making us great, and He WILL make you a blessing. So when nothing seems to be going right, look to God and the things of God. Trust, you will see a change. God will provide you with what you need in order to obtain what it is He has preordained for your life. If you don't settle for less, you will see what greatness God has for you. Family, there is HOPE in Christ Jesus. Hold on and gain enough strength to make it day by day if necessary. Know that God has a plan for ALL of our lives and it's better than any plan we could have ever hoped, dreamed or thought of for ourselves. Be patient and wait on God! Have a blessed life, family. I pray that the Word brought forth to you has lifted burdens, destroyed some yolks, given you enough rope to hold on to to give you the strength to make it.

PRAYER:

Father God, we come to You grateful and thankful for Your thoughts of us are that of greatness. I pray that ALL that I do is a direct reflection of the woman of God You have ordained me to be. Lord, I believe the Word brought forth fell on fertile ground. Let the seeds planted grow and spring forth the best fruit to create the nation You are looking for in all of us. Father God, we thank You for all that You are doing in our lives; we know the end result is of You. Lord, I ask that You continue to cover us in the Blood of the Lamb. I ask that you heal the broken and the sick, in their bodies, minds, souls and spirits. Father, bind the enemy on every hand. I speak LIFE into Your children today. We shall live and not die. Lord Jesus, we are VICTORIOUS in You and we thank You. Heavenly Father, we thank You and count it done in the Mighty Name of Jesus. Amen.

✝ ✡ ☪ ☯

For all the land which thou seest, to thee will I give it, and to thy seed forever.

—GENESIS 13:15

THOUGHT:

Can you imagine that as far as you can see is ALL that you can have according to God. Therefore, if you can't see what's for you, you will cheat yourself out of what God says that YOU can have. Also, it would be commonplace that if you don't have a vision for yourself, you will begin to take what belongs to someone else. Trust, it won't be good for you either. It's like when a woman is ready to be married and she doesn't see her vision nor is she tapping into what or who God has for her, she will have no problem looking at or being in a relationship with a married man. At this point all that is important to her is that she won't be alone and she will at least have a man. But we are all grown and understand that she truly doesn't have him and it definitely will cause more problems than a solution for her and her loneliness. If you let the scripture above marinate in your soul, you will see that God doesn't put limits on what we can have, we do. He says for ALL the land that you SEE. I can see for miles and miles. I can see land in multiple states, I can see land in countries I haven't been to and I can see the island I will own and possess. And if you don't have your own boat, jet or plane, I guess I will see you when I decide to come inland. (LOL, but very serious!!)

Family, stop settling for some of what God has for you and begin to get ALL that He has for you. See all of your success; in your careers, your homes, your relationships, your marriage, as a wife, as a husband, as a mother, as a father, as a BILLIONAIRE!! But, there are some things you won't see if you don't let your lot (burdens) go. Some people/burdens will attach themselves to you, who don't see what you see, They are preventing you from seeing what you should be seeing and preventing you from getting what God has for you. Please grasp that God says, WHATEVER you see, He will give it to you. It doesn't always mean that what you see is of God. That's where your relationship with the Father comes into place. He will speak to you and let you know that what you see and want is of Him. He won't show you something as yours if it is contrary to His Word. He won't show you something as yours and not give you the necessary tools to obtain it. Don't be like David. He saw Bathsheba, another man's wife, and he put it in his mind that he had to have her and in the process of getting her, he committed all types of sin against God to get her. As she appeared to him, know that some things are about to appear in your life. Don't imagine without checking with God first if it is what He wants you to have or not.

The first place the enemy attacks us is in our minds. So it could be a vision of your flesh, which is an enemy to you all day, or if you are a praying individual, you will seek God for the vision to make sure it is of Him and not wishful thinking on your part. In order for you to do this, you must seek a daily relationship with God. I don't know how your relationship is or was with your birth father, but in order for you to communicate with him and know what he wanted from you, you had to spend time with him and talk with him. The relationship that you have built over the years will dictate how you would approach your father for anything. The relationship will give you a sense of what you believe and know what your father wants for you and expects from you. If God is who you say He is to you and I say that He is MY FATHER, my all in all, then without a shadow of a doubt, I know what He wants for me and what He expects from me. I, in turn, live my life in a manner in which to obtain what God has for me. I live my life in prosperity, in love, in healing, in peace, in happiness, in freedom, in caring, in sharing, in believing, in forgiveness and in trust. I live my life in God! Believe God. Believe in the vision God has given to you and don't get it twisted with the vision you decide to feed yourself. Do what's needed to have the vision that God has given you to come to fruition. Know that God will give you what He promised you. Just believe and do your part to obtain it.

PRAYER:

Lord, let Your people not put limitations on the things you say that we can have. Lead, guide and protect us with your all-knowing power. We thank You for the vision You have given us and we bind the enemy from placing anything that he'd have us do in our minds. Lord, there are many of Your people suffering with head issues, causing headaches and neurological deficits, I plead the blood of Jesus on the lives of your children being afflicted with these problems, in the name of Jesus. Lord, we thank You for keeping us thus far. We thank You for the huge vision You have given many of us to see and obtain. Father, we thank You for every day is Father's day because of You. Though society has a tendency to not recognize the work of the father, I give You the glory and honor for providing us with natural fathers. Thank You as these men walk in your statutes and do Your Will in their lives for themselves and their loved ones. It is in Your precious Son's name, Jesus, that we pray. Amen.

✝ ✡ ☪ ☯

VERSE:

Wait on the Lord, and keep his way, and he shall exalt thee to inherit the land: when the wicked are cut off, thou shalt see it.

—PSALM 37:34

THOUGHT:

Ladies, don't think that I left you out to dry as I didn't pull the fellas' cards. For some, if not most of you men keep picking your women based on what you see. You're not seeking God no more for your mate than women are waiting for GOD to send them theirs. It's why the majority of you are in unequally yoked relationships/marriages now. You let the first thing you look at, be the end-all and be-all to what you feel is to be yours. When in actuality, she isn't for you in the first place. But what looks good to you ain't always good for you, as my mother used to say.

I was with a man that I know God sent to me because I mean no harm or no offense, and trust, he knows I wasn't attracted to him in that way. I am partial to my age or slightly older, dark-skinned, big men, the athletic type, preferably footballish and for those who know Anton, know that he didn't fit any of what I just described. We were friends and God allowed me to see him in a new light. What a choice of word; ya'll know I called him my Glow Worm because he is so light and was glowing in the dark the night of my first surgery for breast cancer. The point of the matter is that I had to forget about what it is that Denise wanted, and I listened as God first gave me the vision and then spoke to me that he was who He (God) had sent to me. Then God had me wait for our lives to fall in line with His purpose for us. I can't speak for Anton, but I believe God had to have spoken me into his spirit, as to why he wrestled for years, how we made sense to him and for him. This is nothing but God. The beauty of it is that because I knew it, I trusted everything about our situation. I have given you a piece of me just to let you know that I am in no way, shape or form exempt from the Word. People often ask me, why am I so blunt or harsh, and I answer with scripture, the Word states, it's sharper than a two-edged sword. That's pretty sharp and it will cause a lot of damage and not for your bad. The Word isn't meant to be fluffy, light, sweet and soft. It is meant to evoke change, and anything that is going to go through change has to go through wear and tear, so to speak. We go through the fire to come forth as pure gold. Most things go through a process that will cause pain, but the end result is beauty. Childbirth is painful, but the end result of that pain is life. The end result of the nine-month WAIT is life.

The above scripture suggests that if we WAIT on God and in the process of waiting, do as He commands us to do, He will give us the land. Can you imagine taking a butterfly out of its cocoon before its transformation? We would NEVER get to see its full potential or beauty. As difficult as it may seem, in order for you to get what God has for you, you must wait. Wait on God with as much excitement as you have when you wait on line to see your favorite artist perform. Wait on God as if you're waiting on line to purchase the latest jeans, sneakers or McDonald's Happy Meal. The bottom line is to wait on God to fulfill the vision He has given you and to perform all of the promises He has made to you.

Family, don't miss out on the best that God has for you because you are not patient enough to wait. Are we yet holdin' on?

PRAYER:

Father God, we come to You this morning praying, praising and worshiping You. Forgive us for our sins. Forgive us, Lord, for not waiting patiently on You. Father God, You said it in Your Word that, if I wait patiently on You, You would incline unto me and hear my cries. You said that I shall renew my strength, I will mount up with wings as eagles, I will run and not be weary and I will walk and not faint. Father, You said that You are my God and that You will strengthen me and help me. Thank You for being a very present help in my times of troubles and struggles. We give You the Honor and Glory for it all belongs to You. Help us, Lord, to wait on the promises that You have given us. Help those who desire a mate/spouse to wait on You. Thank You, Jesus, for calling my name. I praise You, I love You, I honor You and I obey You, Lord. In the name of Jesus, we pray. Amen.

✝ ✡ ☪ ☯

Family, there are days that I am in such deep prayer for us that I get a Holy Ghost headache. I know some of you know what this is. Many of us are going through serious afflictions of our minds, bodies, souls and spirits. Spiritual warfare is no joke. Family, the enemy is mad at all of us for receiving God's Word every day. The enemy can't stand our praise. The enemy can't stand us that he is attacking many of us reading and receiving His Word, whether directly or indirectly through someone you hold dear to you that you share it with. Understand that the attack is due to the faith you have in God. The more you trust God, the more the attack is going to come. Put on your boot straps and the WHOLE armor of God, for the enemy is busy and is here to kill us. Family, know that though the Word may not get sent forth to you via this medium, it gets sent to me via God and it is for me to pray without ceasing. Let the blessings of our Father be upon you all today and forevermore. Tell your people you love them, as I love you, as God ultimately loves all of us. Peace, Nise (Denise)

✝ ✡ ☾ ☯

VERSE:

Rest in the Lord, and wait patiently for Him: fret not thyself because of him who prospereth in his way, because of the new man who bringeth wicked devices to pass.

—PSALM 37:7

THOUGHT:

In order to find peace, rest and calm, it sometimes takes work on our part. Unfortunately, the world in which we live in is hectic and it doesn't lend itself to peace and quiet. It creates noise, havoc and uneasiness. But even in all of this, family, I come to remind you that you can rest in the fact that you are in the presence of the Almighty God. He is able to do exceedingly and abundantly above ALL that we ask of Him or think!!! When you feel as though being patient and waiting is an option, I need for you to understand that it is not. For we should not expect a person to do something that we are incapable or not willing to do ourselves. Therefore, if we claim that we can't wait patiently, we shouldn't expect God to patiently wait on us, as He does for the rest of our natural lives. God doesn't get excited nor bent out of shape of our circumstances or our current/past/future behaviors. God is relaxed, calm and is resting as He sits on the throne, patiently waiting for us to return to Him. Who are we that we can't wait patiently on God for whatever it is that we are seeking His face for?

PRAYER:

Lord, we give honor and praise to Your Holy name daily. We come to You, Father, seeking and desiring to do Your Will and exhibit Your way in our lives. Lord, we thank You for blessing us beyond what we can ever imagine, think or measure. Lord, help us to not look to people who do their own thing and appear to prosper. For we know that prospering is more than obtaining things; it is about us obtaining You. Father, for we know without You, we can do NOTHING. We thank You for loving us in spite of who we've been, who we are and who we might be in the future. We thank You each day for waking us up and providing us with the opportunity to get it right in You. Lord, forgive us if we have said, done or thought of anything that wasn't of You. Father, I thank You for rest, calm and patience through my trials and tribulations. I thank You for the level of trust and faith that I have in my heart, mind, body and soul toward You. For Lord, I don't for one second believe that I would be at this level if it were not for You who has been on my side. Father, I never want to take You or the presence of Your love that You send me through Your people for granted. Father God, I thank You for placing each one of the people reading this and their families into my life and heart, that I may love them, enjoy them and pray for them. I love You, Lord, with all that is within me. We bless Your Holy name. Father, heal Your children of ALL infirmities. Let Your loving arms encompass and spare Your children from the hand of the enemy. I pray this prayer and ask these blessings in the name of the Father, the Son and the Holy Spirit Jesus. Amen.

✝ ✡ ☪ ☯

We give thanks to God always for you all, making mention of you in our prayers: remembering without ceasing your work of faith, and labor of love, and patience of hope in our Lord Jesus Christ, in the sight of God and our Father.

— 1 Thessalonians 1:2-3

Just a little Word for us to understand that God expects for us to pray for one another as a part of our faith. Our faith isn't just connected to God through our belief of Him for ourselves, but we must have faith in Him for others as well. That is why when I pray, I pray for each of us. I believe God can do any and all things for me and for all of His children. He is not an exclusive God. He doesn't have respect of persons. I am no more special to Him than anyone else in this world. There are things about me that God absolutely loves, then there are things that He needs to continue to put me through the fire to get rid of to make me completely who He would have me to be. This is His labor of love, hope and patience toward me. If God can have this level of expectation of me, then I must in turn have the same level toward Him, you and myself. I have to wait on Him, for it's about God's Will and way for me.

If it were up to us, we would profess that we are a completed work. I thank God that His work isn't done in us. It is pleasing to know that we can all stand for room of improvement. Can you imagine if your mate was the sweetest person, the thought of that person getting any better than that, would make you melt with joy. It is a beautiful thing to evolve into who God desires you to be. That all begins by us doing as He says we should do; by understanding that you will only get as much out of God as you can believe Him for.

The scripture above suggests that part of His Will for us is to pray for one another, remembering that this is His way of knowing outwardly your faith, love and hope in your Lord in His sight. Therefore, it is imperative that we hold each other up in prayer and have faith that those prayers will come to fruition. When we do this, we are showing love toward one another and God by being obedient to what He has asked of us. We are also exhibiting faith in the things we ask of God not only for ourselves but also for the people that we pray for. It's great to believe in God for yourself, but it's an even bigger deal to believe in God for your fellow man. God wants each of us to live our lives knowing that we can do ALL things through Him. But if you know this scripture, you will know and understand that your faith/belief system is attached to it. It will only manifest, IF you believe in Him. God wants us to understand that if you can believe Him, you can go from defeat to VICTORY from poor to PROSPERITY. Your actions must correspond with your beliefs and your faith. If your actions, which is your faith, doesn't correlate with each other, then you truly don't believe in what you state/claim you are believing God for.

Let's continue to believe God, pray, and have enough faith to know that whatever God says He will do, He will do it! It's not going to be done in our time; this is where your patience, trust and faith have to kick in, but that it will be done when God knows that we are ready for the things we ask of Him. Family, hold on, keep the faith, believe God for more than you could ever imagine and wait on Him to perform it for you. Have a blessed journey in God. I will be praying for us without ceasing!

PRAYER:

Father God, in the name of Christ our Lord, we come to you early with this prayer of faith. We believe You are Who You say that You are. You are our Father, the Father of ALL nations. You are the author and finisher of our faith. We believe by faith, we can do ALL things through You. Because of this belief, Lord, there is no good thing that You will withhold from us. Father, we thank You, we love You and we praise Your Holy name. Let our actions supersede the amount of faith we profess to have. We know that if we have faith as little as a mustard seed, that it's enough for You. But if our actions were to equal that, it may not amount to much. Lord, we ask that You increase our territory. By faith, Father, we are healed. By faith, we are one in You. By faith, the enemy can't steal, kill or destroy nothing that is of You. The enemy can't have our lives, he can't have our children, he can't have our homes, he can't do anything, lest we allow it. Lord, I thank You for allowing me to pray daily for Your people and our expected end in You. I thank You for all that you are doing in my life. Father, I have faith that I am Your workmanship created for good work. Thank You for loving me in the midst of Your love for all of your children. Lord, we ask that You continue to cover us in the Blood of the Lamb. In the name of Jesus, we pray. Amen.

✝ ✡ ☪ ☯

My baby sister, Aliah, has requested that I break down this next scripture for her. She stated that she is late in her request, but it's never too late to inquire about the Word of God nor is it ever too late to receive the Word of God. Baby Girl, I pray this helps in your understanding of this scripture. It happens to be one that I live by. Because all that know me knows that the only concern to me as to who I am, is God! I don't let man rule who it is that God says that I am and will be. Praise His name if you know who God says that you are. Praise His name for not being bound by people and most importantly, by your own thoughts. Be blessed living in FREE-DOM!!!!!!!!!!!!!!!!!!!!!!!!!

VERSE:

Finally, brethren, whatsoever things are true, whatsoever things are honest, whatsoever things are just, whatsoever things are pure, whatsoever things are lovely, whatsoever things are of good report: if there be any virtue, and if there be any praise, think on these things.
—PHILIPPIANS 4:8

THOUGHT:

Many people don't realize that their thoughts need to be healed. Your thoughts are often the product of damaged emotions, traumatic events and of what people have said about you. The greatest gift you can give yourself is self-acceptance. Family, we must learn to look at the world/people in a positive way. Your perception of life and others can create good, positive or negative cycles in your life. Learn how to love yourself and be kind to yourself. You must do this in order to be kind to others. Stop believing negative things people say about you. Better yet stop falling for false images the world puts in front of you. Make yourself better from the inside, then out. Be true to yourself. It helps you to be satisfied with where you are and who you are in your life. It will allow you to be happy and have healthy relationships. Know that every time you make excuses, you are lying to yourself and to God. One of our greatest challenges in our walk with God is to resist the temptation to allow the past and what others say or expect of you determine who you are today. Don't be plagued by haunting memories; you do have control over your thoughts. The above scripture deals with us reprogramming ourselves to think better thoughts. You must choose what you are going to think and meditate on. For so a man thinketh, so is he! And because the enemy knows this, he will destroy your morality, your mind and your life.

Most actions don't start with the act; they start with a thought. Thoughts are like seeds planted and when fed, they grow into all types of things in your life, especially, if you're not feeding your thoughts the right things. Understand that thoughts can turn into motives and motives are about why you do what you do. Do right and think right because it is the right thing to do; it is what God desires us to do. When you pray and do things, pray and do works with a pure heart. Ask God for what you want and think on good things. If you're gonna pray, you need to be praying believing that what you ask for, you will receive it. So erase all of the negativity out of your minds, then ultimately out of your life. Think and live by all that is pure, true, lovely, honest, virtuous and good. Finally, give praise to God for the good in your life. Keep your hope in God's Word that it will become reality.

PRAYER:

Father God, we thank You for free minds. Lord, we thank You that we are no longer bound by man or our thoughts. Lord, for those who continue to struggle in this area, we ask that You cover minds that are held captive by negativity and the thoughts of others. Lord, we thank You for allowing us to survive what we have endured, understanding that it isn't who we are today. Thank You for allowing us to survive what the enemy set forth as a plan to kill us. Thank You, Lord, for the good and pure thoughts that You have toward Your children. The devil is a liar and we know that our mind is his playground. Thank you for instructing us to think on all that is good in order for us to have happiness and be free. Lord, take away the medicines the doctors are placing Your people on for their minds. Heal, touch and deliver, Lord, in the mighty name of Jesus. We praise Your name for the ENDURANCE, THE TRIALS and the VICTORY. We love You, Lord, You are forever our all in all. In the name of Jesus, we pray. Amen..

✝ ✡ ☪ ☯

VERSE:

For I delight in the law of God after the inward man: but I see another law in my members, warring against the law of my mind, and bringing me into captivity to the law of sin which is in my members. O wretched man that I am! who shall deliver me from the body of this death?

—ROMANS 7:22-24

THOUGHT:

Family, there is progress in awareness. When you become aware of what it is that God will have you to do, you begin to move forward in the you that God ordained you to be. Know that when you follow God, there is going to be conflict. Your desire to live Holy is a direct contradiction to your flesh. Living Holy is a spiritual thing. And unless you walk in the spirit consistently, living Holy is difficult and impossible at best!! It's not natural for you to pray and do good to a person who has wronged you. Or as the Word states, do good to them that hate you. What in the WORLD is that all about? Help me, Lord Jesus. Yes, I get stuck on scripture as well. Not stuck to the point that I don't know it but stuck to the point as to whether I am going to practice scriptures that teach us to do this. Pray for me, as I continue to pray for you all. Now back to this Word. Forgiveness isn't a natural thing to man. Please know that without God, it can't be done. As to why I only asked Him to help me, no one else can do it or can help you do it. Following God places you in a position to desire and want to do the right thing while simultaneously another part of you is trying—no, let me correct that—is doing whatever YOU want to do, blaming it on bad habits.

We claim and lay hold to the fact that God has saved us from sin. I can testify that He has done it for me, but that doesn't stop this fleshly body of mine to occasionally revert back to some of my old ways. We are walking a very thin line on this road of salvation. And because God challenges us on the very things we were saved from, this is where we and He can see growth begin. Especially, when the very things He challenges us on don't affect us as it used to. To be transformed and changed is a process. It takes faith, courage, wisdom and patience to see the results that bring out the true nature of Christ in us. It's when we strip down and bare our complete selves to God and ask Him to bring about the necessary changes that we need to make in order for us to experience God's true power. At this point, God is transforming us from being superficial to supernatural with Him.

As I live day to day, praying and thanking God for deliverance and His continued daily work in me, I find it easier to walk the straight path that God has put before me. I know that I was lost in myself and now I've found not only myself, but I found GOD in the process of gaining freedom! I stand fast today and prayerfully forevermore in the liberty wherewith Christ has made me free.

PRAYER:

Lord, I thank You for this Word. The mind is a terrible thing to waste and I refuse to waste it on negativity, worry, fears or on those that may have offended me. Father, I thank You that when and if I fall that You have given me the tools and permission to get back up again. Thank You for being a God of not only a second chance but of infinite chances. Only You know the number of times You will tolerate us moving in our own accord. I thank You for my living in obedience to Your Word. Lord, thank You that I am free today where no chains, no situation, no illness nor no man has me bound. My spirit, heart, soul, body and MIND belong to You. Bless us, Lord, that we may ALL walk upright before You. Thank You, for continuing to work in my life. I am grateful that I am a work in progress and that You are not finished with me yet. I pray that when my time is near that You will be able to say to me, "Well done, my good and faithful servant." I pray for my entire family, I pray for our leaders, I pray for those who are lost and don't know You today. I pray for those who don't have faith. I pray for the wounded and brokenhearted, for I was once where they are. Father God, give us the strength to endure this present world. We humbly ask these things, seeking Your face in prayer in the mighty name of Jesus Christ my Lord and Savior. Amen.

ABOUT THE AUTHOR

Denise Y. Barrow is a Registered Nurse of twenty-six years, specializing in Neonatal Intensive Care. Her many years in the field have allowed her to deal with the psyches of a multitude of people from all walks of life. A field where death is prevalent has given her the opportunity to counsel parents of neonatal loss as a member of the bereavement team. She later suffered the neonatal loss of her daughter, Nyleve, in 1991. Denise, like others, is no stranger to surviving hardships.

Denise is a native New Yorker born and raised in Brooklyn's tough Albany Projects where she kept herself busy making doll clothes and writing plays for puppets that she made. Denise has always enjoyed expressing herself in creative ways whether it's designing or making clothing, drawing, painting or delving into home design. She attended the School of Visual Arts and Fashion Institute of Technology. In 2000 she embraced her writing skills and contributed to the anthology, *Ghettover Girls: In The Words of Sisters In Their 20's. Denise's Daily Word* is her first solo book publication.

In 2005 Denise was diagnosed with Stage 4 breast cancer. It was during this time that Denise took to pen and paper even more due to her family's and friends' concern for her health. In order to provide comfort, she wrote to them daily to encourage them with the Word of God—by sharing scriptures and breaking down the meaning of shared scriptures in her own vivid words, based on her experiences, compassion and her unwavering wit. To further ease their minds, she wrote to them weekly to give them updates on her treatments, the doctors' reports and on how she was feeling.

It has been ten years since Denise's cancer diagnosis. It has been a long road to healing and recovery, but it hasn't stopped Denise from continuing to share her faith as she continues to minister to people over the phone, via emails and texts with her positive spiritual encouraging words. These are often mixed with humor and her undoubtedly straight-from-the-hip real-talk approach. She writes as if she's speaking directly to you in person. Her love of God and His Word via the Bible excites her and grants her all that she needs to live her life thankfully, gratefully, joyfully, happily and in peace. Denise currently resides in GA.

You may email the author at dybdesigns@aol.com.